With God's Oldest Friends

PASTORAL VISITING IN THE NURSING HOME

Henry C. Simmons
Mark A. Peters

Paulist Press ◆ New York ◆ Mahwah, N.J.

Cover design by Tim McKeen.

Excerpt from "Burnt Norton" in FOUR QUARTETS, copyright 1943 by T. S. Eliot and renewed 1971 by Esme Valerie Eliot, reprinted by permission of Harcourt Brace & Company.

Excerpt from ALICE'S ADVENTURES IN WONDERLAND & THROUGH THE LOOKING GLASS by Lewis Carroll, New York: Airmont Classics, 1965, is reprinted with permission of Thomas Bourgey & Company, Inc.

Library of Congress Cataloging-in-Publication Data

Simmons, Henry C.
    With God's oldest friends : pastoral visiting in the nursing home / by Henry C. Simmons, Mark A. Peters.
        p.   cm.
    ISBN 0-8091-3636-8 (alk. paper)
    1. Church work with nursing home patients. 2. Pastoral theology—Catholic Church. 3. Catholic Church—Clergy. I. Peters, Mark A. II. Title.
BX2347.8.N87S55 1996   96-6
259'.4—dc20   CIP

Published by Paulist Press
997 Macarthur Boulevard
Mahwah, NJ 07430

Printed and bound in the
United States of America

Contents

94024

*For Helen McDonald and Kay Peters,
from whom we have learned much about
friendship and compassion*

Introduction

$\mathcal{A}$ rabbi friend dropped by my home the other day. We were out, so he left his card. On the back he had written, with his typical wry good humor: "Dropped by for a pastoral visit. Sorry you weren't home. Will return in three years." Some days that's the way we would like to deal with nursing home visitation.

Nursing homes can be very uncomfortable places for the outsider. For most of us, the best we can hope for regarding nursing homes is that we will not end our days in one. Even now, when our health is strong, nursing homes can remind us in no uncertain terms of the frailty of life, and may offend us by their violation of cultural norms of what is beautiful and important. But—and this is a big "but"—the conscientious pastoral minister knows that pastoral visitation in the nursing home is required. Parishioners will ask, "Have you been to see my mother yet?"—and there are only so many times we can answer, "Not yet, but soon." More importantly, the desire to do what is right, to be a faithful pastoral minister, and to reach out to all one's parishioners are powerful incentives to consider effective nursing home visitation.

Thus this little book. It assumes that the pastoral minister wants to do what is required in a pastoral charge and do it well. It assumes that the pastoral minister wants to be competent in pastoral visitation. It assumes that the world of the nursing home is a largely unknown world. It assumes

1

that fear of the unknown and a sense of incompetence will be alleviated if the pastoral minister is introduced step by step to this new world.

When we wrote this book, we had very specific "ghosts in the corner" (the people we were addressing). They are pastoral ministers, bright, devout, and caring, for whom the world of the nursing home is largely a mystery, but who are willing, even eager, to learn in order to better serve "the least of these." Thus, there is no sense whatsoever of talking down or addressing the reader from a moral high-ground. We are eager to share what skills and insights we have so that people in nursing homes are better served by pastoral ministers, and so that these pastoral ministers are better prepared for pastoral visitation.

These pastoral ministers may be clergy, lay church-professionals, laity who have undertaken this special ministry, Protestant or Catholic, women or men. Anyone in ministry may experience a level of discomfort in nursing home visitation. Few theological schools or programs of lay ministry have adequate preparation for this particular ministry. Churches mirror, in large measure, general social attitudes: the "cultural ideal" is young-looking, strong, and productive—hardly the description of most nursing home residents. Churches, eager for growth, emphasize ministry to young families and youth. Few churches have any kind of serious educational programs for older adults or systematic programs of chaplaincy for nursing home residents.

Various plans to accomplish pastoral visitation in the nursing home by using occasional and untrained lay visitors rarely seem to work adequately. We have all heard tales of parishioners who complain at the end of a hospital stay that "no one from the church visited me," when in fact there was a steady stream of visitors from the church—but not a member of the ministry team. This is also the case for nursing home visitation, and not without reason. The pastoral minister is seen as the one charged with the care of souls; he or she has occupied a central place in worship and pastoral care; and it is the pastoral minister who has to provide continuity of care in difficult and critical times in the spiritual growth, nurturance and care of people in the final stage of life.

Part of the difficulty with providing adequate (or, even better, excellent) pastoral care in the nursing home has to do with dramatic shifts in the way we die in old age. Until relatively recently (the late 1940s) antibiotics were not available and old people died of the "old person's friend"—pneumonia or some other infectious disease. It was often quite possible to care for someone at home because the time of illness or disability would be relatively brief. Today, most of us can expect to die of degenerative disease rather than infectious disease. Except in the case of AIDS, people now die of primary causes (that is, some primary organ failure) rather than of secondary causes (for example, a virus or bacteria). People die *much* sicker. Not only do more women work full-time outside the home (thus limiting the home care-giving that is available), but people take so much longer to die and, as they are much sicker, require extensive care—often with such difficult and personal items as toileting and bathing. In this context, nursing homes are a new phenomenon, meeting new needs, often on a for-profit basis. The next chapter describes nursing homes in some detail, but first a word about another part of the difficulty in visiting a nursing home.

Nursing homes can be scary places for the outsider. Most of us are very uncomfortable with sick people; and many of us find ourselves at a time in life when our parents or their friends are beginning to show signs of frailty. They may be well at the moment, but we have wondered with some dread how we will take care of them if and when they will need help. Like our parishioners, we will feel very guilty if, in their need, we "abandon" them to nursing homes to be cared for by strangers. We recognize that at this juncture the women among us will be saddled with a disproportionate amount of caring; that old sibling rivalries may make it difficult to decide which of the adult children ought to take the lead in coordinating care; that society makes those who "fail" in their filial duties (by letting a parent go into a nursing home) feel great shame; that our own parents may—in their terror of life in a nursing home—play on our deepest sense of guilt. Nursing homes, which we view as outsiders, can raise fears about what lies in store for us at the end of life.

One seminary professor told us that visiting a nursing home has fueled in him a powerful drive to be sure that he will never wind up in a nursing home. He was being honest, if not realistic. Nursing homes can bring us up short as we contemplate the probable shape of the end of life. In Colonial America, the Puritans constantly reminded people that life was short and that death was always close. Funerals were thus important public and religious events, reminding all to pray to be saved from a sudden and unprovided-for death. Today's common wisdom describes the best end of life we can hope for as many good years in active retirement ended by death in one's sleep (with no previous period of disability). The nursing home reminds us that our probable fate is not such a death.

Our fears, however, do not paint an accurate picture of the very human reality of life in a nursing home. Nursing homes can add *years* to life. One denominational nursing home group got into terrible financial trouble because they used general actuarial tables in computing what to charge in up-front fees. What they found was that the people in nursing homes, because of the excellence of care, lived on average from seven to eleven years longer than their counterparts who did not have this nursing home care. Nursing homes can add years to *life*. For many new residents there is a sense of relief, freedom, creativity, and gratitude in having access to much-needed care. G. Janet Tulloch is an eloquent advocate for nursing home residents. She chose to enter a nursing home twenty-five years ago so that she could live a full life in spite of cerebral palsy. Her column, a regular feature of *Aging and the Human Spirit*, is a witness to a full, committed, passionately-lived human life. She is not alone.

Nursing homes do present unique challenges. They introduce those who live there and we who visit to powerful challenges that are at heart spiritual—that have to do with the growth of our souls. Visitation there pushes us to see that our public "high noon" vision of the human (well-adjusted, strong, healthy, young, productive) is very partial indeed. It pushes us to see that people with very severely disabling conditions can be leading authentically human lives, touched by moments of joy, by the challenges of accepting life in a nursing home as their moral career, by moments of growth in generosity, and—at least for some— by a contentment that has no bitterness, and by a love of God that is beautiful (and perhaps humbling) to encounter.

Indeed, without in any way romanticizing the nursing home, we could make a case that the pastoral minister's personal spiritual life can be both nourished and challenged by pastoral visitation there. The nursing home is a place for a prophetic ministry of pastoral minister to resident that redefines what is of value in life. It is also a place for a prophetic ministry of resident to pastoral minister that redefines what is effective in a ministry of spiritual growth.

The order of the book is this: Chapter 1 gives a brief history of nursing homes and explains what is involved in present day homes—how they are organized, what facilities are available, the three levels of care, some specialized vocabulary used in nursing homes, how they are administered, who does what, when, where, and how. Chapter 2 invites you to be intentional in your approach to nursing home visitation, making decisions about whether you are doing pastoral care or pastoral counseling or some of both. Chapter 3 introduces the practicalities of a normal nursing home visit. Chapter 4 introduces pastoral visitation to residents in special units, in particular to those with dementia and to those in hospice units. Chapter 5 speaks about special cases—when the person is asleep, or sick, or unresponsive, or asks special favors. Chapter 6 addresses the need for and use of rituals, including communion or the Lord's supper. Chapter 7 addresses ways of making more graceful the transition of parishioners from their own homes to nursing homes. It may seem more logical to have put this final chapter at the beginning—a parishioner makes a graceful transition into a nursing home, and *then* we begin the process of visitation. We chose to put it at the end because we believe that the ability to guide a parishioner well in such a passage depends in large measure on knowing the life of a nursing home intimately.

One brief stylistic note: when referring to a nursing home resident we use either "he" or "she" rather than the more awkward "he/she." We use the female pronoun much more often than the male pronoun, however, as a reminder that the vast majority of people in nursing homes are women.

We hope that your time *With God's Oldest Friends* will be for you a time of grace.

1. The Nursing Home

A. Background

The term "nursing home" has a very specific meaning, namely an institution that provides twenty-four hour skilled nursing care at an intermediate (i.e. non-hospital) level. However, in popular usage the term refers generally (and often imprecisely) to a variety of institutions or "homes" where people—usually thought of as the old—are given care. In this chapter we will give a very brief background of the term, and will sketch out what it means today, both narrowly and broadly.

For people whose memories reach back into the early part of this century, the term nursing home brings up horrible pictures of the "poor house" on the edge of town overlooking the town cemetery where the poor, the poor old, and often the insane were housed. Even for those born considerably later, nursing homes were "houses of death" where medical care, staffing, and even physical setting were widely reported as terrible. These images were often reality based, and their memories linger on. A friend tells about trying to explain to his grandmother that she could only get the care she needed in a nursing home. Her impassioned and thoroughly negative reply ("I worked hard all my life and no one is going to put me into the poor house to die") shows some of the power of long memories. Let us

look at the reality old people remember that makes them
very apprehensive about nursing homes.

In the early part of this century, most of the people who
lived in state pauper institutions ("poor houses" or "county
homes") were old. Without a pretty vivid imagination it is
difficult to picture the conditions these people lived in.
While the state took some responsibility for the care of those
who could not take care of themselves and had no family to
care for them, this provision was not—to put it mildly—
generous. The undeserving, the abandoned, the disabled,
the handicapped, the aged, widows with children, orphans,
the feebleminded, the deranged, the chronically ill, and the
unemployed were grouped together. Indeed the poor and
the insane were often housed together. Medical diagnoses
were often crude. With limited understanding of psycholo-
gy and even less understanding of aging, conditions that are
now routinely treated in the old were misdiagnosed. People
were grouped together on the basis of their common pover-
ty rather than that their physical or mental conditions indicated that they belonged together.

What is equally important is that many of these elderly
had few or no immediate family to look out for their best
interests (a situation that may still be prevalent among
some institutionalized elderly today). All in all, the associations with the term nursing home (namely, poor, old,
insane, without family) for people whose memories reach
back to this time tend to be extremely negative.

The 1974 publication of Robert Butler's Pulitzer Prize-
winning *Why Survive: Being Old in America* was a landmark
for the field of older adult studies. While the picture painted by Butler of nursing homes then showed they were better than the poor houses at the turn of the century, there
was still plenty of bad news. In his chapter titled "Houses
of Death Are a Lively Business," Butler tells some real hor-
ror stories. A few homes were excellent, of course, but they

were the exception rather than the rule. Butler visited nursing homes himself (sometimes in disguise) to observe the conditions first-hand. The gory details are not important (although for those who want to pursue this, Butler's book is still widely available). Suffice it to say that he found everything from deficiencies in the physical plants themselves (fire hazards, lack of evacuation plans and/or training, etc.), to deficiencies in staffing (inadequate numbers, inadequate training, poor pay resulting in high turnover rates, etc.), to deficiencies in medical care (poorly trained doctors and nurses unfamiliar with the health needs of geriatric patients, inattention by staff to medical needs, drugs used as restraints).

The picture, while better in some areas and homes than in others, was still pretty bleak. The image of nursing homes among the general public was not improved by newspaper reports and first-hand accounts. These powerful word-pictures still have their effects today. People who had to place a family member in a nursing home in the mid-1970s (the time of Butler's book) still have hard memories. A family might have placed a father in his eighties in a nursing home because they could no longer care for him at home. For a variety of reasons, the family was never happy with the way he was cared for in the nursing home. Now when one of the then younger generation needs nursing home care, there is likely to be high resistance. When my own father was suffering from a deteriorating heart condition, his doctors wanted to admit him to the same facility in which he had placed his father twenty-five years before. No matter how much that facility had changed over the years and no matter that it now had a unit devoted to cardiac rehabilitation—which was what my father needed—he adamantly refused. The memory of the poor care his father had received was stronger than any new reality we could try to show him.

B. The Modern Nursing Home Industry

In 1971, the federal government mandated that states license nursing home administrators. This, in conjunction with the introduction in 1965 of Medicare and Medicaid, was to have long-term consequences for nursing homes. For one thing, Medicare and Medicaid created an adequate financial basis for nursing homes, allowing them collectively to become an industry. With the possibility of making a profit, many corporations went into the nursing home business. Thus, far more proprietary (that is, for-profit) nursing homes were built by corporations whose first-line commitment was not even necessarily anything in the medical field.

The government began to get substantially involved in the nursing home industry through Medicare/Medicaid financing and requiring licensure of nursing home administrators. Within a few years, other legislation was passed requiring, for example, that homes providing health care must have at least one registered nurse on duty at all times (a condition Butler had found to be rare). States had to have a certification procedure for nursing assistants requiring training and a test administered by a state agency.

While there remains much to be done to improve conditions in the nursing home industry, the industry has come a long way in a relatively few years. The leadership for much of the change appears to have come from inside the industry itself. Medicare/Medicaid legislation that opened up the field to for-profit development brought with it competition that has turned out to be something of a mixed blessing. The quality and quantity of services offered by top-of-the-line facilities whose clients can move or be moved to another facility has widely improved. But in many that deal largely with Medicare/Medicaid recipients, there is an incentive to cut corners, with unsafe and/or unsanitary conditions as a result. Nevertheless, the overall picture has improved substantially since 1974.

Not-for-profit nursing homes (which includes most denominational homes) refers to homes run by church agencies, fraternal groups, charity groups, etc. The development of modern denominational not-for-profit homes pretty much paralleled the development of for-profit homes. Parallels even run to chaplain services: some for-profit and some church-run, not-for-profit nursing homes have chaplain services; conversely, many for-profit and many not-for-profit nursing homes, including some church-run nursing homes, have none.

C. Varieties of Retirement and Nursing Home Facilities

In popular usage, retirement and nursing home facilities are often spoken of in the same breath. However, there are clear distinctions to be made depending on which *levels of care* are offered—independent living, assisted living, and/or intermediate nursing care. In the rest of this chapter we will describe several residential options for the elderly. We then will define and describe facilities with independent living, assisted living, and/or intermediate nursing care. We indicate what you, the pastoral visitor, will encounter in the independent living units, assisted living units, and nursing care units or facilities.

1. *Continuum-of-Care or Total-Care Facilities*

The trend in the industry at present favors the building of facilities that incorporate all three levels of care—independent living, assisted living, and health care. These tend to be upscale. The finest (and usually most expensive) retirement facilities are continuum-of-care or total-care facilities, usually found in suburban areas, often close to shopping, entertainment, etc. but not so close that traffic from those areas might spill over into the facility. Some of these started out in areas that have grown up around them, but often have sufficiently large campuses that they can offset unwanted encroachment.

These top-of-the-line facilities tend to be either proprietary or denominational homes open to those who can afford to pay for them. These homes offer three levels of care: independent living, assisted living, and health care. This arrangement is referred to as a "continuum-of-care." Usually such total-care facilities require a large lump-sum payment for entry.

2. Free-standing Nursing Homes

Many nursing homes are not part of a continuum of care. These nursing homes, whether for-profit or not-for-profit, have been designed specifically to offer intermediate nursing care. These nursing homes offer not only twenty-four hour skilled nursing care but a variety of services and care for people who need more than occasional help (such as in assisted living units) but less than hospital care. Nursing homes may be located anywhere, although they are more likely to be in metropolitan or suburban than rural areas. People often come directly from the hospital or an assisted living unit to a nursing home. In all cases, the measure of excellence is simply the extent to which the nursing home adds to the quality of life of its residents.

People often do not get to choose the nursing home they will be in. Especially if a person is covered by Medicare and is being transferred from a hospital, that person must accept the first open bed in whatever facility accepts Medicare patients. A person in this situation may be forced to accept a placement that entails geographic separation from family and friends. Most intermediate care facilities (nursing homes) have a waiting list. Even if a person is on the waiting list for a particular facility, a sudden change in health conditions could result in a placement elsewhere.

3. Apartment-Style Complexes for the Elderly

At least in newly built facilities, probably the most common option is apartment-style complexes for the elderly. These offer a variety of apartment arrangements and available services depending on client need and ability to pay. Costs can vary greatly, although such facilities are ordinarily substantially more expensive than ordinary apartment facilities of comparable quality. Many of these now have health care units into which apartment tenants can be admitted for short-term stays or while waiting for a permanent placement in a nursing home.

Top-of-the-line group residential or housekeeping apartments may offer a large variety of services, including a small bank, a store, and an on-site doctor/dentist office. They usually offer a large range of activities and educational programs. The "budget" units in this category may offer fewer services, charge for some services that top-of-the-line units include in general fees, and may offer more limited activities and educational programming. Some of these may rely heavily on local church and volunteer groups to supply much of the activity.

These complexes will often be located in suburban areas, though some can be found in rural areas (usually government subsidized), and many of the budget units may be located in urban areas.

4. Adult Homes

Another option that we mention only in passing is the "adult home," often referred to as "board-and-care" or "mom-and-pop" operations. These are often located in older homes, and house eight to twelve persons. They supply very little (or no) medical care and few structured activities. Some areas of the country have very few of these operations and there is a definite trend away from them in most locations, possibly because they are seen as a last resort for those who can afford nothing better. This does not have to be the case, however. The intimate scale of such homes could well offset the advantages of an institution. There are a variety of experiments, some very successful, with group homes or congregate living arrangements that maintain an at-home, familial atmosphere. Such experiments should be encouraged.

5. *Home Care*

Care in one's own home or in the home of a loved relative is almost always the dream and the first choice of the frail. It is sometimes the first choice of the spouse or adult child who is the caregiver. In the best of all worlds, it would be hard to imagine anything better than being cared for in familiar surroundings by family. Certainly, where there are adequate human, financial, and medical resources for home care, home care has enormous advantages.

We do not live in the best of all possible worlds. Home care over an extended period of time can be very burdensome for the caregiver financially, physically and emotionally. Resources are usually very limited; people have jobs to attend to; other family members make demands; it is not easy to put one's own life on hold. Few health-care plans reimburse adequately non-professional care given at home no matter how much it adds to the health and well-being of the person cared for.

Even with very limited resources, home care is sometimes the only option available. In the course of your ministry you will encounter home caregivers who, in spite of heroic effort and good will, are exhausted by offering care—without adequate support—for which they are not trained. Some communities offer home nursing care, respite care, and/or adult day-care. These may relieve some of the strain. In our experience the ability to give prolonged home care to a very sick person without exceptional resources is extraordinarily demanding. Two pictures come to mind simultaneously. One unforgettable picture is of a friend who cared for his wife, an Alzheimer's sufferer, for seventeen years, together maintaining her dignity and his throughout. The other picture is standing outside an adult day-care facility at 7 am, watching people arrive on the way to work with a very frail parent, already bathed, fed, carefully clothed...and seeing this same person on the way home from work at 5:30 pm picking up the parent for an evening or weekend of care. The latter picture makes us grateful on many levels for nursing homes.

D. The Three Levels of Care

1. Independent Living Units

Independent living units are the first stage of total-care facilities—the most upscale of the institutional options available. (A one-bedroom unit might have an entrance fee of $100,000+, with monthly fees of $1200. On the very low end of the scale, a one-bedroom entrance fee might be $75,000 and on the high end $150,000.) Obviously, the majority of people who can afford to move into these homes come from a very specific economic bracket, although many not-for-profit facilities offer "scholarships." Unlike the purchase of a townhouse or condominium in the general community, the unit does not pass on to the resident's heirs. Rather, it reverts to the complex when the person dies or has to move to the next level of care.

What motivates people to pay the large up-front fee many of these facilities require? Usually, individuals enter a facility's independent care housing while they and their spouses are still in fairly good health—indeed, most facilities require prospective residents to enter independent living units where they must be able to function without assistance. The advantage of this arrangement is that residents get to be established and to be known while they are reasonably healthy and able to care for themselves. Later, as health deteriorates, they can move to the next level of care—assisted living. Then, if they reach a point where they need continual health care, they receive priority on the waiting list (which most have) for bed(s) in the facility's health-care unit. Thus they can be relatively assured of not having to relocate to a new facility because of changes in health. A further substantial benefit of moving into a total-care community is that there is an obligation for lifetime care by the organization, even if the individual runs out of money. Other reasons for making such a proactive choice may include one of two other conditions. First, one (of a couple) may suffer a deterioration in health. The spouse may not feel able to take care of self and spouse. Or, they may feel capable, but maybe anticipate that any further deterioration in either's condition would result in a forced move. To avoid having to make the move under the pressure of necessity, the couple may move voluntarily before circumstances dictate it, allowing them time and resources to deal with the move. A second reason may be the loss of a spouse. The surviving spouse may opt to move into a total care facility for companionship and support.

Physically, independent living units are typically either free-standing cottages or townhouses, or apartment suites located on the campus of the retirement complex (but normally not attached to the assisted living or health-care center). Most maintenance of the unit (usually including interior maintenance) and maintenance of the grounds is the responsibility of the complex. Individuals may have some leeway in decorating and outdoor gardening, but usually not much.

You may be visiting parishioners in this type of environment. Normally one approaches people in these units as you would a private residence. There is no gate or guard or person that you need to check in with, but contact with the parishioner prior to going to visit is both a courtesy and a way to avoid missing them if they are out. These are usually fairly active individuals who are able to get to church on their own. They continue to participate in many of the same organizations and activities they were involved in before moving into this community. The activities planned for the people living in assisted living and health-care units are usually open to them, and there may be events planned specially for them. But, for the most part, these people remain part of the mainstream of society. One of the more touching moments we have encountered with people in independent living was at a denominational retirement complex where people from the independent living units came into the health center at meal times to help feed those people who needed assistance. Some people in independent living units, however, have an unholy terror of the health-care unit and may even refuse to visit friends who have moved there.

2. *Assisted Living Units*

When health deteriorates to a point where independent living is no longer possible or sustainable, residents move to assisted living units. In assisted living units there is a level of care appropriate to the needs of the resident that is less than skilled nursing care. Moving to an assisted living unit is a mixed blessing. There is relief at getting needed help, but there is also the real decrease in health that occasioned the move. As a pastoral visitor, you will hear expressions of gratitude for needed care as well as some real sorrow at a loss of independence and health. Family members, however, sometimes report that they only hear the shadow side of the move.

The decision to move to assisted living is based on an assessment of physical needs, described in terms of "Activities of Daily Living" or ADLs. These are activities we take for granted, but which in the absence of the ability to perform them seriously impair independent living. Principal among ADLs are feeding, toileting, bathing, speaking, walking, dressing, and so on. Guidelines will vary from facility to facility, but at all facilities there are guidelines about which ADLs and how many ADLs a person can require assistance with before they are no longer considered suitable candidates for assisted living. Obviously, some carry more weight than others. For example, needing help with bathing or meal preparation is not in the same category as needing help with toileting.

People in assisted living usually live in apartments or rooms that vary in size and layout for differing needs. Larger facilities normally offer more choices. Services offered at this level will depend on the operator's philosophy about helping people maintain independence. Some facilities will do as much as they can to help a person stay in assisted living as long as possible. Others will go by a strict set of guidelines without variance, but we will discuss those shortly.

One of the main services associated with assisted living is communal meals. Most multi-level facilities that have an area designated as assisted living (as opposed to simply apartment complexes for the elderly) have a communal dining room and require people to eat at least one meal a day there for nutritional as well as social reasons. More meals are optional (at greater cost) but usually one meal taken by all residents is enough to support a food service. Some older complexes may not have cooking facilities in the assisted living apartments and all meals will then be eaten in the communal dining room (unless the person chooses to dine out which at this level they should be free to do). If a person fails to come to eat, a staff member would normally go to check to make certain that person has not fallen or suffered some other injury or incapacitation.

Many people in assisted living units remain fairly active. At this point, most have given up driving but facilities usually provide some type of van transportation to shopping locations, churches, etc. Many of these people are quite able to take advantage of this van service. Also, there is usually a full calendar of activities going on within the facility itself (the larger the facility, the more in number and variety).

Other services may be offered at this level, some free and others for a charge. In the first category, there may be limited nursing care. This might involve dispensing medicine from an infirmary. One facility I have visited will sometimes send the nurse to an assisted living apartment with medication if that will help to keep the person out of health care a little longer. Other minimal nursing care may be available as well, for example physical therapy for which the person may not be separately billed. Many retirement facilities are incorporating on-site physical therapy into their programs. Other services for which the person is not specifically charged may include (but surely are not limited to): activities, library, chapel, sundries store, communal garden, etc.

Services that might be available on site but for which the person would be expected to pay extra include: maid, laundry, beautician/barber, bathing assistance, care generally provided by nursing assistants, medication, doctor's office, dentist, etc.

Visiting people in this setting will not be exactly like visiting in the independent environment. While you should still have free access to assisted living residents, you will probably pass a receptionist's desk at the main entrance.

Employees will be moving around the area (they should be wearing ID badges). You will pass many people as you move down the hallways. Individual rooms are private, but access is not. It is at this level that you will start seeing the more frequent use of walkers and wheelchairs. Some assisted living units do not allow people who are wheelchair bound, but most do. Walkers and wheelchairs may also foreshadow an inability to perform ADLs that will necessitate a move to the nursing home or to intermediate nursing care.

3. The Nursing Home

In a total-care facility, people move to the nursing home either from assisted living or, if they have had serious illness or surgery, from the hospital. Residents in nursing homes have a wide range of abilities. Some are the well elderly who have no chronic or terminal disease but who need assistance with ADLs. For example, they may be mentally fully alert, but may not be steady enough on their feet to go to the bathroom alone and may only be able to bathe themselves with assistance. Some residents in nursing homes are, for lack of a better expression, temporarily ill. Not that when they recover they will leave the nursing home (though for a variety of reasons that may be becoming more common); rather, they are bedridden, perhaps confused or unresponsive due to illness, medication problems or a variety of reasons. When their condition is remedied or stabilized, they will likely return to their "same old self."

But this level of care does also have what is probably the popular image of the "typical" nursing home resident. These people may be chronically ill. They may be what is termed the "frail elderly." Some of these people may be genuinely and permanently confused. Some will have slow cancers. Some will suffer from the effects of strokes. How residents and staff respond to the frailty within and around them varies considerably. In the best nursing homes, all are actively engaged in living (or, when appropriate, in dying), as you will see when you visit. In one wonderful nursing home we visit, the elected head of the Residents' Council, Mr. Samuelson, is 102 years old. He fully expects to be re-elected next year. Given the quality of skilled and human care in that facility, he probably will live to run for office again.

Most of the rest of this book is about nursing home visitation, so we will leave a more detailed description of pastoral visitation for the following chapters. Our final word in this chapter is about the quality and size of nursing home facilities.

E. Quality and Size of Nursing Homes

Simply put, there are good and bad, big and small nursing homes. There are some horrible places out there. The combination of the profit motive and the fact that many elderly who end up in these homes don't have immediate family to serve as advocates for them has created some bad conditions. But in the face of the same realities, there also are some "unfancy" nursing homes that provide good to excellent care. In every type of nursing home there are people who work hard to make their clients lives as pleasant as possible, just as there are people who—for a variety of reasons including low pay, poor training, and poor staff morale—give care that is at best marginally adequate.

The question of size of facilities is probably a more important question than appears on the surface. An institution that houses fifty, or one hundred, or two hundred non-related residents has inherent limitations and strengths. There often are attempts to make the appearance of these facilities homey. Sometimes the attempt is sincere, and that sincerity is reflected in the decor. But it remains obvious, despite any well-intentioned affirmations to the contrary, that the nursing home is not (a) home. The more compassionate and forward thinking facilities try to accommodate as many personal belongings as possible in the nursing home, but in residents' rooms, most often shared with a roommate, there is limited space and only a limited amount of personal property can be kept. Usually, all that remains are photographs, some wall-hangings perhaps, maybe a chair and television.

Working against creating a homey atmosphere is an economy of scale. Normally, the more nursing beds in a facility the greater the return on investment. Large scale facilities (especially if owned by a corporation that owns multiple facilities) create greater buying power. While there is an advantage to this, there is a line that divides an appropriate economy of scale from an impersonal large scale that fosters impersonal care.

Whatever their limitations, nursing homes are integral and important institutions in our society. They are, at least to this point, the best way we have found to care for those who are frail and cannot care for themselves or get adequate care in a familial setting. There are many nursing home staff who try nobly to make life as pleasant as possible for those in their care. We have seen frail elders flourish once they have made the initial adjustment to a nursing home. We have seen many frail elders who find there a place to live responsibly, to care for others and to grow in wisdom and in grace.

2. Planning, Preparing, Responding

A favorite few lines from *Alice in Wonderland* are instructive for nursing home visitation. (Alice is speaking to the Cheshire Cat.) "Cheshire Puss, would you tell me, please, which way I ought to go from here?" "That depends a good deal on where you want to get to," said the cat. "I don't much care where—" said Alice. "Then it doesn't matter which way you go," said the Cat.

In your nursing home visitation, it is important to have a clear idea where you want to go—that is, to be intentional in this part of your ministry as in any other part. Just as you take other aspects of your ministry seriously, thinking about them, planning, preparing, so you need also to approach visiting the institutionalized elderly with an equal purpose.

In this chapter, we will suggest two major approaches (with many variations) from which you may choose. We will then look at the three key elements that go into your choice of approach: the needs and capabilities of the residents, your strengths and gifts, and the work done by other staff.

A. Pastoral Care or Pastoral Counseling?

Basically, you have two options in your approach to residents in the nursing home, much as you have with the rest of the people for whom you are pastoral minister: pastoral care or pastoral counseling. What is the difference between the two approaches and when is one more appropriate than the other? Let's distinguish (without going into great detail) what we mean by pastoral care and pastoral counseling, and add a word on a ministry of intentional presence.

1. Pastoral Care

Pastoral care—with all its splendid variations—is what you do most of the time with most people. Pastoral care in the nursing home might involve *spiritual direction*, helping those you visit find devotional material that best suits them, sharing scriptures, discussing their worship experiences with them, helping them to discern God's will for them or God's presence in darkness. It may involve praying with the person you are visiting, or helping the person learn to pray or to meditate. The elderly—even people who have been lifelong church members—may not know how to pray, or be comfortable with praying. It is a wonderful gift to be able to work with people who may just now be finding an openness to a more intentional prayer life.

Particularly in the loneliness that may come at the beginning of life in a nursing home, what pastors can do is to help new residents in nursing homes to pray—to develop the inner side of a life of devotion so that they can live through to assurance, to the re-creation of a meaningful life, and to a new relationship with God. There are some print resources that may be helpful. For example we have found helpful a little book by Susan Coupland, *Beginning To Pray in Old Age* (Cambridge, MA: Cowley, 1985). But print resources alone are not enough. You yourself have to be willing to be a guide whose qualifications are rooted in a serious struggle with the same ultimate realities and some sureness of knowledge about the inner life of prayer. There is no doubt that this may test the depth of our own life of prayer, the adequacy of our meditation on the mysteries of faith, and the quality of our own inner lives.

You might also be called on to help a nursing home resident make an *ethical decision*, regarding anything from remarriage to death by suicide. Everyday ethics tries to answer the question, "How then ought I to live?" In the nursing home, the context in which the resident now lives is different from the non-nursing home world; the questions are sometimes urgent, sometimes new and puzzling. T.S. Eliot has some wonderful lines that speak of this time of life: "O dark dark dark. They all go into the dark [...] As we grow older The world becomes stranger, the pattern more complicated Of dead and living" ("East Coker," in *Four Quartets*). Part of pastoral care may involve helping people answer the question, "How then ought I to live?"

A specific set of questions may arise regarding power of attorney, medical power of attorney, and living wills. Here, there are other usually resources within the nursing home for the person (and yourself) to draw on. However, the residents you visit might ask your opinion as a "theological expert" to assure themselves that what they are doing is acceptable within their religious tradition. These can be complex but unavoidable questions that may take research on your part.

You may provide care through participating in *educational programs* at the nursing home or by doing bible study with the person or persons you come to visit. Within the nursing home you will find so many levels of awareness, interest, and education that education can be a daunting task. On the one hand, you don't want to speak down to residents. There are, as we said, people in the nursing home whose minds are wholly intact and whose interest in a wide world has not been diminished by their need for some help with ADLs. If these people were active in Sunday school or adult education, they will probably relish some "meaty" programs. Less able—but still functioning people—might profit from something like the *Bless Bible Studies: Bringing Life Experience to Scripture Study* (Minneapolis: Augsburg Press, 1988). This four part bible study has a leader's manual and large-print participant leaflets. Issues addressed include trust, faith, friendship, anger, being cared for, preparing for death, God's promises, loneliness, suffering, comforting, value and worth. An earlier text, *In Wisdom and the Spirit: A Religious Education Program for Those Over Sixty-Five* (New York: Paulist, 1976), highlights other issues of importance in its five units: the phenomenon of aging, the priesthood of the elderly, prayer and spiritual life, reconciliation and eucharist, and death, dying and resurrection. Together these two texts give some indication of the scope of educational issues that can be addressed.

As you might expect, *liturgy and preaching* are major areas for pastoral care. If the person or people you visit can come to church occasionally, this should be arranged. If not, you might consider planning with the chaplain or activities director to lead a liturgy from time to time. (Later we will talk about working with people who are mentally incapacitated; for the moment let's focus on nursing home residents who are mentally able.) As you prepare your reflections or homily, it may become clear to you that you need to take into account the special needs, circumstances, and interests of your congregants. What you would say to the well people in the parish may or may not fit. Special needs and interests will become more apparent the more you visit, as you and the residents together try to understand God's will and God's call to them to "abundant life" in these special circumstances.

2. Pastoral Counseling

The second option you may wish to take as a model from pastoral visitation is pastoral counseling. Factors differentiating pastoral counseling from pastoral care include the length of time and depth with which a specific issue is addressed, and the "contractual nature" of the relationship. Let's look at these one by one. First, "time and depth." Pastoral counseling may be of short or long duration— from several visits to an ongoing relationship. The key here is that a specific issue (or cluster of issues) is engaged intentionally over time with a depth appropriate to the expected insight or resolution. Second, pastoral counseling has a "contractual nature." There is a mutual expectation about roles and assumed expertise. The counselor has the right to probe, to ask questions, to draw on theories of personality and socialization. The person with whom the counselor is engaged in counseling has a right to expect confidentiality, an appropriate level of expertise, and the capacity for sorting out the agenda the counselor brings to the relationship.

Residents in nursing homes have, of course, problems like other parishioners. What may give their problems particular urgency includes the clear sense of limited time to resolve important issues (present or from the past) and the enclosed—and thus in some way "hot house"—nature of their living situation. Because of loss and grief, self-esteem and empowerment can be key issues in their relationships with family members, staff, and others. Anything that might minimalize the seriousness of possible problems might lead us to try to apply band-aid therapy to major wounds. Two books we have found helpful in this area are *Empowering Older Adults* by Elinor Waters and Jane Goodman (San Francisco: Jossey Bass, 1990) and *Compassioning: Basic Counseling Skills for Christian Care-Givers* by Margaret Ferris, CSJ (Kansas City: Sheed & Ward, 1993).

We have already indicated a number of possible counseling issues. Some of these will be short-term, some long-term. Short-term pastoral counseling might be called for in helping a person deal with grief over some loss (a common element of life for people living in a nursing home). It might be called for when there are issues of self-worth in difficult circumstances. It might mean helping them deal with roommates, other residents, or staff—all people whom they cannot avoid even though they might not like them or get along with them. It might entail helping them to get on with their lives, that is, helping them to adjust to their new living arrangements and to look for ways that they can continue to affirm their personhood.

Some of these may not seem as if they can be solved in a few weeks. Some of them will never be totally resolved. You may concentrate on one of these issues for several consecutive meetings. It might then be a sort of sub-text in your planning for other work with this person, and may be dealt with more indirectly as other issues arise. In all short-term counseling, however, there should—as much as possible— be an understanding about what needs to be achieved for the counseling to end. How about long-term pastoral counseling in this setting? Without oversimplifying the issues, why not, and where better? Some of your people are going to live here for years. You will have an opportunity to visit with them regularly over that period of time. It may be now, in these circumstances, that they need your help in developing themselves as persons and in dealing with baggage from the past. While pastoral counseling will not always be appropriate, desirable, or desired, you may have no better opportunity for productive pastoral counseling than you might find with one of your people in a nursing home! One recent book by T. Hargrave indicates the shape a particular form of long-term counseling might take: *Families and Forgiveness: Healing Wounds in the Intergenerational Family*. (New York: Brunner/Mazel, 1994).

3. A Ministry of Presence

Somewhere between pastoral care and pastoral counseling stands a ministry of intentional presence. In its simplest form, it is "just being there." Sometimes that may be what any parishioner needs most. For the person confined to the nursing home, this may be even more so. You will not always have to have the right thing to say, the answer to deep mysteries, or the latest information from the congregation. Sometimes just showing up will be the best care you can give. Sometimes this ministry of intentional presence may include listening to "old stories" as people reminisce.

What specifically makes this ministry of intentional presence stand between pastoral care and pastoral counseling is the skill and understanding you bring to the situation. For some older adults, the process of reminiscing, even in an informal setting, may have certain innate value. Study in the area of the intentional use of reminiscence has indicated that some older people need to reminisce in order to maintain ego integrity, or to "solve" the past, or to find the threads and patterns of behavior that make their lives make sense. Reminiscence may be an important work for an older adult (although it may appear to us on occasion that their reminiscences seem to have some historical inaccuracies).

On occasion, even these apparent historical inaccuracies can be a helpful starting point for conversation as people try to retell the past, deliberately or not, in order to understand the present. I once worked with a group of quite frail elders for several weeks, facilitating their conversation, hearing their stories, being present. Again and again a theme that emerged was the great gap in family values and social integrity between the "good old days" and today. The fifth time we met I said, "It seems that you inherited an intact world of family and neighborhood, and you are leaving behind a 'ruined' social order. How does that make you feel?" In the conversation that followed, we all were able to listen to each other, to hear sadness and even guilt, and to support the process of "solving" the past.

The ministry of intentional presence may take many forms. It stands between pastoral care and pastoral counseling, and relies for its effectiveness in some measure on the ability of the pastoral visitor to be an active listener. For those who would like to pursue a formal process of reminiscence, we recommend *Guiding Autobiography Groups for Older Adults* by James Birren and Donna Deutchman (Baltimore: Johns Hopkins, 1991).

B. Choosing Appropriate Approaches

In determining what method or approach you will use in your pastoral visiting, we will now look at the three key elements that go into your choice of approach: the needs and capabilities of the residents, your strengths and gifts, and the work done by other staff.

1. Needs and Capabilities of Residents

A hard but rewarding question to ask youself is what you think these nursing home residents are capable of. From what we have already said, it is clear that we believe many of them are capable of a great deal of learning and growing. We believe that, ordinarily, aging older adults are still capable of learning anything they could have learned earlier in their adult years. They may learn more slowly—or more quickly; motivation to learn and change may be lesser—or greater. Illness, poor eyesight or poor hearing, or the complexity of a technical task may slow the learning process. But it is likely that we may have to remind not only ourselves but them that they can still learn.

Pre-conceived notions of what the elderly are capable of certainly affects our approach to them. We are in a culture that teaches us to "read" a person's worth by what we see. The character, strength, and beauty of some nursing home residents may only become clear to us with time, as we "see past" their frailty to the hidden depths within. This is certainly better than writing them off as of little capability because of physical limitation.

What *is* God's will for old age? Why has God let some very frail people live so long and what is God's call to them in this part of life? There are two enormously different, diametrically opposed, and competing visions of old age. The first sees the end of human life as decline and failure. This is the prevailing view of mass American culture, which adores youth. The other vision—less compelling, perhaps, but more true to the spiritual traditions—sees enlightenment as the goal and end of human life. For Christians, one articulation of this goal or end of human life is "eternal light." All die into the light. This could be seen primarily as a reference to the afterlife. But there is also the possibility that this refers to God's call to all to be united profoundly in love with God—that we are all called to mystical union with God. Either interpretation of the invitation into the light sets up a powerful mandate for pastoral care—we are present as guides of the person into eternity and/or we are present as companions on the journey into God in this life, just as they are to us. The title of a recent book by J. Thibault captures some of this drama and promise: *A Deepening Love Affair: The Gift of God in Later Life* (Nashville: Upper Room, 1993).

We do not have to come completely to terms with our own aging to be able to work with the elderly. We must, however, at least be aware of the issue of how we feel about it and how those feelings can positively or negatively affect our interactions with the old, and be able to definitively reject the vision of old age as just failure and decline. Ideally, we will be led by our work with the elderly to more fully explore that dynamic and will, and, through that, find visiting them to be a personal growth experience as we together journey into God.

There are a variety of approaches that we can take to visiting with the institutionalized elderly. No one approach will work for everyone, though some may always be unacceptable. Those that are unacceptable are those that start from false suppositions on our part and tend to treat the people we visit on the basis of generalizations or stereotypes that we hold about the elderly. While there may be some general characteristics of the aged that apply across a broad spectrum, the aged are no more (or less) of a homogeneous group than any other subset of our culture.

2. Your Strengths and Gifts

The best rule of thumb for choosing a method for working with people in nursing homes is to remember that they are each unique individuals, loved and called by God, with individual needs and circumstances. Then you must assess your own strengths and gifts. If they are individuals, so are you an individual. Allowing that our answer to the call to serve God's people may motivate us to learn new and specific skills, we each have our own limitations, also given to us by God. Thus, we must ask ourselves: What can I realistically expect to be able to do?

This is not to be seen as an excuse to avoid further education or to excuse us from trying new and different ideas. However, we do need to ask ourselves questions about available time, specific skills, and overall aptitude. Time is always a factor in a pastoral minister's life. There are many demands, and nursing home visitation is a demand—like so many others—that cannot be done both effectively *and* quickly. Again, we simply encourage you to be intentional in planning your visits so that time is well used and time limitation does not become an excuse for doing nothing.

If time is a limiting factor, our specific talents are of importance. Some people may have skills and gifts that makes visiting seem easy (at least to the onlooker). Others may feel that their gifts lie elsewhere, and they may have to work harder at developing the necessary visiting skills. At some level, gift or not, you will have to develop the ability for nursing home visitation. However, if you feel you are stronger in education, or liturgical preparation, or social outreach, or some other area then you might want to spend more time sharing that particular gift in the nursing home. You might find something in your particular strength that you can adapt to your visitation style which will make you more comfortable. Be bold and be patient.

We should take ourselves into account in formulating our approach to visiting in the nursing home.

3. The Staff

In planning our visits we also ought to take into account the skills and talents of staff whose work we do not need to duplicate and whose insights can make our work more effective. Most nursing homes have on staff trained social workers, activities directors, etc. These persons' services are usually available at no extra fee to the residents in the facility. Social workers are usually skilled in counseling; many run growth groups, grief groups, and so on. Activity directors may go far beyond "fun and games" to running reminiscence groups, structuring poetry writing workshops, or supervising a variety of other activities that nurture the human spirit. Some of these people—like the nurses' aides who do so much of the hands-on care—may also provide comfort and care that goes beyond their job descriptions. Staff may also be useful allies in helping us use our time where it is most needed. Without abdicating our own responsibility and insights, we can often learn from them who needs our pastoral visit and for what particular reason.

This does not minimize or replace what you have to offer. You are the residents' best and most identifiable contact with their home church, the community of faith in which they have been nourished in the love and service of God. You have skills in pastoral care and counseling that are specific, and you are charged in a particular way with the "care of souls." The particular training and skills you bring—however much they may vary from person to person—are essential.

Without going into great detail, we have discussed above (or at least hinted at) different approaches or techniques for visiting (some of which we will describe in more detail in the next three chapters). Is there one approach that is better than others? As you might guess, there are those who say yes and those who say no. Those who say no basically maintain that no single method is always preferable. Each method has pros and cons, and one might work better with Mr. Smith and another with Mrs. Jones; but no one way is always to be preferred. Others, not unlike secular counselors have either developed or been trained in a particular approach. We cannot settle that issue here. What we can advise is that you try different approaches until you find what works best for you and for the individuals you visit with. If one approach seems to work for you in all (or most) cases, then stick with it. But be prepared to adapt or drop it if need dictates.

C. Conclusion

In your nursing home visitation, it is important to have a clear idea where you want to go—that is, to be intentional in this part of your ministry as in any other part. Just as you take other aspects of your ministry seriously, thinking about them, planning, preparing, so you need also to approach visiting the institutionalized elderly with an equal purpose.

In this chapter, we have suggested two major approaches

(with many variations) that you may choose from: pastoral care and pastoral counseling. We then looked at the three key elements that go into your choice of approach: the needs and capabilities of the residents, your strengths and gifts, and the work done by other staff. We are now *finally* ready to walk with you through the door of the nursing home.

3. The Basics of Nursing Home Visiting

*I*n this chapter we address some basics of normal nursing home visiting: when to visit, preparation, staffing patterns and contacts, roommates, physical limitations (impairment of hearing, vision, speech, thought) and the pattern of the actual visit. If some of this seems too basic (for example, when to visit), be assured that we do not mean to insult your intelligence. We assume that you (or those with whom you will be working) have little or no exposure to this type of environment and we are trying to answer all your basic questions.

A. When Do You Visit?

If you have not visited a particular nursing home, it is worth calling to ask about the best times to visit. Most institutions have schedules and rhythms. Many nursing homes serve all their residents breakfast in bed or in wheelchairs, between seven and eight. After everyone has eaten, the nurses aides begin helping those who cannot dress themselves. Normally, all people will be up and dressed by ten o'clock unless there are medical orders or conditions that require bed rest. A call to the home, and specifically to the nurses' station for the area where your parishioner lives, can save you from arriving at a time scheduled for a bath, physical therapy, an outside doctor's appointment, etc. Although many elderly are early risers, and although many of them might be at their sharpest in the early hours of the morning, institutional scheduling usually (although not always) means that you have to begin your visit after ten o'clock.

After you have visited the person a couple of times, you will learn the schedule of the facility and of the person you are visiting. You can then work out between yourselves the best time to visit. Just as with people in the hospital, nursing home residents often feel as though everybody else is making decisions for them. If you let your parishioner have some say in when the visits will be, you will be starting off on very positive footing.

How much time you should set aside for the visit depends on several factors—the number of people you plan to visit, their condition, the presence of family, the type or purpose of your visit. Your experience will be your best teacher in this.

B. Getting Focused

In the previous chapter we encouraged you to be intentional in your approach to pastoral visiting in the nursing home. Visiting the institutionalized elderly should be a deliberate pastoral activity. It can be rewarding, and it is very likely to be challenging. Before beginning the visit we find it helpful to spend a few moments in prayer, focusing on the compassion of Christ. If the facility you are visiting has a chapel, you might spend a few quiet moments there. If it does not have a chapel, find a quiet space where you can focus your attention. Be attentive to God's presence; ask for strength and guidance. Remember why you are visiting. Some days you will need every resource at your disposal to be effective in pastoral visitation. Prayer is an important resource.

C. Contact with the Nursing Home Staff

1. The Nurses' Station

We recommend that you begin your visit at the nurses' station of the unit where your parishioner is located. Nursing home residents may receive visits from whomever they choose, and you do not need staff permission (unless there is a quarantine sign posted on a person's door). But while "reporting in" is not a requirement, it will be to your benefit.

Introduce yourself to the professional staff who take care of the person you are visiting. Occasionally, there will be an RN (registered nurse) at the nurses' station. However, especially during daylight shifts, the nurse in charge of the unit will more likely be an LPN (licensed practical nurse). In larger facilities the RN will be in a supervisory role and the LPNs will be the ones who work most closely with your parishioners. Some facilities are now utilizing a charge nurse's aide. This person supervises the NAs (nurses' aides), giving them their daily assignments and acting as liaison between them and the LPN. She (most of the staff you encounter will be female) will probably be at the nurses' station most of the time. The nurses' station is also the place where residents' charts are ordinarily kept. This makes it a center of activity within the institution and is a good place to meet casually the activities' director, social workers, dieticians, etc. All these are people who interact with the person you are visiting. Very few of them will ever be less than delighted to have you visiting.

Telling the staff whom you are visiting gives them a chance to give you information you may need. Staff can usually tell you about physical problems that might affect your visit (such as hearing loss, stroke, poor eyesight, mental confusion, etc.) and what has been happening in the person's life recently both in the nursing home and outside it. In return, especially at first, it is good to let them know that yours is a routine pastoral visit (if such is the case). It may be that clergy visits are so rare that the staff assumes you have come to give the resident bad news. If that situation does arise, the information should be passed on to the staff as well (within the bounds of ministerial confidentiality).

2. Other Staff

You will meet the other staff who are important for the care of the person you are visiting in less formal ways— nurses' aides, dietary aides, orderlies, and housecleaning staff. Some of them have more impact on nursing home residents than some of the professional staff. In particular we mention the nurses' aides.

The NAs (many of whom do wonderful and difficult work) are among the lowest paid people in the institution. One can hear disgruntled NAs asking why they should stay in the nursing home where they are so badly paid. Yet these underpaid, often undertrained and usually overworked, individuals normally provide over ninety percent of the hands-on care for people living in health-care units of nursing homes.

Some NAs have gifts for working with people and have learned much over the years. Only recently have nurses' aides been required to have any kind of specific training and certification. Even at that, personal experience as a NA leads me to believe that the certification test could be passed in some states or localities by less-than-qualified people. If an outside agency (such as the Red Cross) does the training and testing, there is some assurance that standards will be a bit higher. If the home itself does the training, the test by itself may not weed out less qualified individuals.

If NAs work regularly with a person, they can generally tell you not only about physical conditions but about the person's whole situation. Many who have worked as NAs for any length of time see their work as a ministry of encouragement. They do much to get to know and help the people they serve. Anything that you can do to recognize their contribution and empower them will have a direct impact on the quality of care received by everybody they care for in the nursing home.

D. The Visit

We may seem to be taking an inordinate amount of time getting your visit started, but the process sometimes is slow, particularly if you have to deal with a resident's roommate and/or with physical limitations of hearing loss, speech difficulty, and vision loss.

1. The Roommate

After you have introduced yourself to the professional staff and have located the person you are going to visit (residents aren't always in their rooms) you go to your parishioner's room only to find her roommate also there. If this is only a casual visit, or if the roommate is not alert, this might not be a problem. However, if you have come for a genuine pastoral visit and the roommate is not only alert, but feels like involving herself in the visit, there clearly is a problem. (The "interfering" roommate's intent may be far from malicious. She may have a genuine interest in the person you are visiting—after all, she sees her every day.) Your pastoral duties to your parishioner demand that you make every attempt to assure her the same quality of visiting time you give to people who come to your office.

The first option to consider is whether the person you are visiting is willing and able to move. Most modern facilities have lounges or solariums where you may have more privacy, and most people are glad to get out of their room for a while. If the solarium is not available or is in use, there may be a chapel or some other designated space available.

If neither your parishioner nor the roommate is able or willing to move, excuse yourself, return to the nurses' station, and explain your situation. It is possible that they will be unable or unwilling to help—the roommate has a right to be in her room. But usually the staff have enough knowledge of and rapport with the people they care for that they can suggest some solution. They may be able to convince the roommate to leave the room to join an activity. Or they may be able to convince or enable the person you are visiting to leave the room for the visit. Staff generally can and will be very helpful.

If all else fails, drawing the privacy curtain may be your only option. Most rooms in health-care units have curtains (like hospital rooms) that can be drawn between beds. However, this will not provide for a private conversation, will not shield you from a truly curious roommate, and will not block out a loud television or radio. This type of situation requires flexibility and patience.

2. Physical Limitations

There are some common situations you may encounter that will affect your style of pastoral visiting: hearing loss, speech difficulties, and vision loss. While people in health-care units sometimes have good hearing, speech, and sight, this is more the exception than the rule. People who are in health care have had some physical loss or deterioration, often accompanied by decreased hearing and/or sight, some speech impairment, or some combination of these.

A. HEARING LOSS

Hearing loss is common in the very old. Sometimes it can be greatly compensated for by hearing aids, sometimes not. If the person you are visiting is hard of hearing, we offer these suggestions:

- Talk at a moderate rate.
- Do not shout. This can confuse the person and sound like anger.
- Do not change subjects quickly or frequently.
- Make sure the person is aware of your presence before you begin speaking—don't "sneak up" on him/her.
- If a person's hearing is better on one side, position yourself on that side.
- Always (for all visits) sit down to talk. Do not stand looming over people in their beds or chairs.
- Adjust your speech patterns to compensate for a physical problem, not a mental one. Most of these people are hard of hearing, not mentally impaired.
- If there is a "speech board" available, ask the staff for help in using it to communicate.

Finally, don't assume everyone in the nursing home is hard of hearing. More than once I have gone into a room and addressed a person in the same manner that I used in the previous room, only to be reminded gently (and sometimes not so gently) that this person's hearing is fine.

B. SPEECH DIFFICULTIES

Speech difficulties occasionally accompany hearing loss; sometimes they occur as the result of a stroke or other illness. This may be the most difficult handicap to deal with because most of the burden of making communication clear is on the sufferer. Here are some guidelines for visiting a person with speech difficulties:

- If the person is trying to make speech more intelligible, let him/her struggle to get the word out. Do not try to anticipate what is going to be said.
- Lean toward the person to hear better what is being said (a good listening posture to adopt anyway).
- If necessary, ask the person to repeat what was said, explaining that you truly want to understand.
- Don't assume you understood if you are not sure. Repeat what you think the person said and ask for verification. Why talk about the mountains if the person is trying to tell you she has been depressed lately?
- Do not assume that intellectual capacity is diminished. Especially in stroke patients, intelligence may not have been affected by whatever caused the speech impediment.

C. VISION LOSS

The other common communication problem we encounter is partial or complete vision loss. Again, do not assume that someone who is blind is also deaf or simple-minded. You may not have to change your speech patterns. But there are some things you should keep in mind.

- Be careful not to startle the person by entering the conversation too quickly or too loudly.
- A gentle touch can help the person to know that you are still present during intervals of silence.
- Do not be afraid to talk about times prior to the loss of sight.

- Be ready to describe what the person cannot see (e.g. the kind of day it is) if you are asked. This is not morbid.
- Offer to read the mail, the newspaper, the bible, etc., to them.

D. THE BASIC PATTERN OF A PASTORAL VISIT

Many years ago, in an article now long lost, I read a statement by Fr. John Shea, theologian and priest of the Chicago archdiocese, about the basic pattern of liturgical worship: greet the people, speak the word, share communion, send them home. I have thought about this pattern often in preparing to lead worship. We have also found it useful for understanding the dynamics of a pastoral visit. We suggest that every visit have this basic pattern, or rhythm if you will.

The first movement is *the greeting*. This can be brief for someone you have known for a long time or as extensive as the time it takes to introduce yourself to someone who has never met you before this day. In whatever form it takes, it entails directing your attention wholeheartedly to the person, and creating a hospitable space in which you and this other person come together in the name of Jesus Christ. "Wherever two or three are gathered in my name, there am I in the midst of them"(Mt 18:20). Sometimes, it helps to say these words of the gospel aloud or at least to let them flow through your mind and heart.

The second part of this rhythm is *speaking the word*. This term may sound overly liturgical but it adequately represents what happens in the visit. Two Christians have come together. The word they share is their common ground. If one of those two is a pastoral minister or spiritual leader to the other, then the sharing of the word is not only an appropriate image but an integral purpose of the visit. Proclamation of the word is central to all gatherings of Christians. In these visits, we share the word by listening, by encouraging, by consoling, by challenging. We may share the word of the scriptures explicitly, as that is appropriate. We share ourselves in service to the people we visit. Sometimes we share the word in silence because human words fail. "Through our inarticulate groans the Spirit is pleading for us, and God who searches our inmost being knows what the Spirit means" (Rom 8:27, NEB).

The next movement is *sharing communion*—coming to a moment of intensity and depth in God's presence. As John Shea was speaking from a liturgical and eucharistic perspective, he clearly meant "communion" as eucharist. Our primary reference here is not communion as eucharist (although that may indeed be part of a visit). Rather, we are referring to the depth of relationship that can result with someone with whom we share the word. "Communion" in this sense might take the form of a prayer, of a spoken word or shared silence, of a touch, or of an assurance of God's forgiveness. Whatever it is, the person needs to know for that moment that she *matters*, that God loves her and that you are there for her. This will occur more easily and naturally the more often you visit with a particular person.

The last movement ("sending them home") refers to *ending the visit*. If we can be allowed to continue our liturgical analogy, we might call this the blessing and dismissal. It entails some form of closure on what has been discussed during that visit and some form of looking ahead to the next. In many situations, a formal blessing is an appropriate last word, with the sign of the cross, perhaps traced on the forehead.

Even for a brief but intentional visit, this is a good framework. If you think in these terms even when you are only stopping for a few minutes, we believe that the people you visit will find your visits more satisfying. With enough presence and intentionality, the four steps might be very brief indeed. For example, a *very* short visit might be this:

The greeting: Turn to the person with full attention, say hello, and call the person by name. *The word:* Say something as simple as, "I hope today is good for you." Or you may say something like, "One of my favorite psalms is 'The Lord is my shepherd, there is nothing I shall want.' Or, one of my favorite prayers is, 'Our Father.' Do you have a favorite?" *Communion:* You might say something as simple as, "God cares about you; you matter to God," or, taking the person's hand as appropriate, "God loves you and is here with you, even in the hard times." *Ending:* Perhaps the simplest is, "God bless you" or "God be with you," with the sign of the cross. On paper this may look artificial, but it is a useful framework. We invite you to try it out for yourself.

E. Time

It is up to you to make clear to those you are visiting how long you have to spend with them. Often this is as simple as saying, "I'm here to be with you for fifteen or twenty minutes." Sometimes it is important to let the person know this is not the time for a regular visit. An extended example may help. I am currently visiting several men at a local facility. I visit one day a week, spending fifteen to twenty minutes with each of three of them one week and the same time with the other two the next week. The men know that I will be with each of them for that time every second week. But I also try to stop and see each one every time I am in. For the men I am not seeing that day I usually greet them, tell them immediately that I am in to see other people and have just stopped by to see how they are, and remind them that I will be visiting them longer next week. If something of significance came up in their last visit, I might mention this briefly, or if I promised them something I will repeat my promise. I then say I have other people to see, and excuse myself. Most of the men have been appreciative of these brief visits between times and of my forthrightness in saying how much time I have at the moment.

Sooner or later in your visiting, some lonely person in the nursing home whom you do not visit is going to ask you to visit with them. This can be heart-wrenching. What do you do? Sometimes a smile, a pat on the hand, and a kind word will suffice. Some people, however, will be more persistent. There are two ways of extricating yourself from this situation. First, you may simply say, "I'm sorry, I do not have time to visit with you"—and go on your way. This may seem surprisingly cold, but it is honest. You cannot visit everyone; you are finite; you have other obligations (even to yourself). Second, in order to get free at this moment, you might say, "I'm sorry I don't have time now, but I will visit with you the next time I come by." This may *seem* more kind—particularly if the resident seems "out of it" and unlikely to remember. This second option we do not recommend at all—unless you really intend to honor your promise. It is not honest, and, more often than not, the person will remember and will try to hold you to your promise.

If you feel there is a genuine need for more pastoral visiting at a nursing home (and there almost always is), you might speak with your fellow pastoral ministers, especially at ecumenical gatherings, and encourage them to visit their parishioners in the facility (if they are not already doing so). You might also try to get some pastoral ministers (professional or lay) to volunteer time to come in to visit people who don't regularly get pastoral visits. Finally, you might try to organize a lay visitor program. All these options are worth trying, and each meets different needs in different ways.

After you have finished your visits, it is a good idea to report out to the staff at the nurses' station. This may mean nothing more than saying goodbye and thanking them for any assistance they gave you or simply for taking care of your parishioner. This gives them an opportunity to speak with you or to ask you a question. These simple courtesies are welcome and important.

Now that you have said your goodbyes to your parishioner and the staff, have made it past all the people in the halls, and have stepped back out into the light of day, take a reflective moment to commend all these people—residents, staff, and yourself—to God. "When I was ill you came to my help, when in prison you visited me" (Mt 25:37 NEB).

4. Visiting in an Alzheimer's Unit

*I*n this chapter we discuss pastoral visitation in Alzheimer's units, with a brief word about hospice units. We describe the units, examine the stages of Alzheimer's disease and the behaviors of Alzheimer's sufferers, describe appropriate ways of responding, make suggestions for the visit itself, and conclude with a reflection on the mystery of God's will in this disease.

If you are able to do so, it is best to visit often enough in the regular units of the nursing home to be comfortable with pastoral visitation there. You may not be able to do so, of course. If one of the people you are already visiting is transferred to the Alzheimer's unit, you will probably want to "walk the walk" with that person. If one of your parishioners is admitted into the nursing home and is put directly into the Alzheimer's unit, the family will need your pastoral skills to help them cope. Part of this will involve actually visiting the person in a closed unit. Virtually all our attention in this chapter is on visitation with parishioners who suffer from Alzheimer's disease and related dementias because of the special impact of these diseases. The other special unit (hospice) is probably much more familiar to you from hospital visitation. Even if it is not, you will find its atmosphere much easier to cope with.

A. Special Units

1. Hospice Units

Hospice units are less common than Alzheimer's units but are being developed with more frequency. Generally, at least in larger nursing homes, you will find both kinds of special units. Hospice units are usually for residents of the nursing home who are in the final stages of a terminal illness. These people are less likely to be the frail elderly; often they are surprisingly young and alert. Hospice units in nursing homes, like hospice units in hospitals, are designed to help those who are dying from terminal diseases to die in as graced a manner as possible. The staff is trained to be comfortable with death as part of the life process, to help the patient manage pain (even with drugs that might not be used so freely in other situations), to help celebrate the moments of life that remain, to help the person and the family speak freely about death, and to be with the dying person in every step of the dying process. Hospice units are deliberate and even celebrative in their approach to death. In our experience they provide a tender and human context for pastoral visitation. Some of what we say about caring for the dying in a later section will be relevant for ministry in a hospice unit. However, if you have a parishioner in a hospice unit, you might want to work with the facility's chaplain or ask a staff member for special guidance in this situation.

2. Alzheimer's Units

The other special unit you will encounter is the Alzheimer's unit. Actually, not every person on the Alzheimer's unit will have Alzheimer's disease (AD). Some will be suffering from what is called organic brain syndrome (OBS—a catch-all diagnosis for people who suffer deterioration of mental processes for undetermined reasons). However, the similarities between the two conditions (AD and OBS) are such that differentiation is not usually necessary. You may also find persons with conditions other than OBS or AD in this unit. For example the Alzheimer's unit may, on occasion, include people who need close medical supervision and who are inclined to wander away from the facility.

Closed Alzheimer's units are either locked or alarmed to keep the residents from wandering away unnoticed. In very rare cases the door may need to be unlocked for *entrance*, by key or by a four-digit code on a key pad. The purpose of requiring a key or code for entrance is to control or monitor visitors to the unit. Normally, a key or code is only required for exit from the unit. This allows easy access for staff and visitors but is sufficient to stop most disoriented individuals. While locked doors are the most common means of keeping Alzheimer's sufferers from wandering, some units are *alarmed* rather than locked. There is a monitor at every exit that signals an alarm (sound or flashing light) when it is activated by the bracelet or anklet worn by the residents. The alarm (which continues until it is deactivated) alerts the staff that someone is trying to leave the unit. We even know of one women's unit in which the exit door was neither locked nor alarmed but simply marked clearly with the symbol normally found on a men's washroom.

Alzheimer's units have staffing patterns that are different from regular units. Not only are they likely to have more staff, but the staff will usually have special training. AD persons especially need qualified staff who understand the nature of the condition and how they are likely to respond. People suffering from Alzheimer's need extra attention and extra kindness to help them function at the highest level of which they are capable. Skilled staff can facilitate this. Conversely, if AD sufferers are treated incorrectly, they may become agitated or even combative.

3. *Mixed Units*

Some facilities are not large enough to have a special unit for Alzheimer's sufferers, who are then mixed in with the general population. In this case all people, regardless of condition, are housed in the same area(s). At least one facility of which we are aware has, in extensive consultation with residents and staff, made a conscious and deliberate decision *not* to segregate people with Alzheimer's. Here, people remain in the room they originally moved into as long as humanly feasible. While a person may have to be relocated for safety reasons, there are no specially designed or designated closed units. All floors or wings house a variety of people with a variety of conditions. The logic of this decision is quite wonderful. The residents decided that they would rather put up with the disruptive behavior of an individual with Alzheimer's than themselves risk being moved away from familiar surroundings and people should they be afflicted with the disease too. In a mixed unit, an alarm system will alert staff when anklet/bracelet wearers pass the monitor, although the regular residents and staff can come and go freely.

B. Alzheimer's Disease

In this section, we will speak about the stages of Alzheimer's disease and about appropriate responses to the kinds of behaviors that might be encountered in a closed unit. Our descriptions are brief. If you wish to explore this further, there is no book better than *The 36-Hour Day: Revised Edition* by Nancy Mace and Peter Rabins (Baltimore: Johns Hopkins, 1991). This book is a family guide to caring for persons with Alzheimer's disease and related mind-affecting illnesses, and memory loss in later life.

1. Stages of Alzheimer's Disease

The brief description of the symptoms of the disease quoted below from *The 36-Hour Day* is chilling. The first paragraph, which is prelude, describes what the individual and the family have endured. The second paragraph describes what you see in varying degrees in a closed unit.

> Later, impairments in both language and motor abilities are seen. At first the person will be unable to find the right word for things or will use the wrong word, but she will gradually become unable to express herself. She will also have increasing trouble understanding explanation. She may give up reading or stop watching television. She may have increasing difficulty doing tasks that once were easy for her. Her handwriting may change or she may walk with a stoop or shuffle or become clumsy. She may get lost easily, forget that she has turned on the stove, misunderstand what is going on, show poor judgment. She may have changes in her personality or uncharacteristic outbursts of anger. She will be unable to plan responsibly for herself. [...]
>
> Later in the illness the person becomes severely impaired, incontinent, and unable to walk or may fall frequently. She may be unable to say more than one or two words, and may recognize no one or only one or two people. She will need nursing care [...and] will be physically disabled as well as intellectually impaired. (284-85)

It is the human face of the disease that is so disturbing: I was part of a small group who helped care for a priest friend from the early stages of the disease until we could no longer care for him ourselves. At fifty-five, this formerly brilliant and proud man needed help with eating, bathing, and toileting. We would often find him sitting in the corner, reading quietly—with the book upside down. Later, in the years he was in an Alzheimer's unit, we saw him—this man whose command of language was spellbinding—lose language. The last coherent thought he expressed, though, was, "It's better it happened to me than to you young people who have so much promise." We saw him grow unaccountably angry or sad; we had to feed him; we had to help him walk even short distances; we saw frustration so enormous it convulsed his body. But we also saw him smile in recognition of a friend, saw him reach out gently to another sufferer, enjoy the feel of the sun or the fragrance of a flower, relax under the skilled care of a nurses' aide, saw him wince at the repeated screams of another resident, join in haltingly in a familiar prayer after all other language had gone, suffer days that were a terror to us—and, we suspect, to him—and die a death that seemed years too long in coming. These are parts of the world of the closed Alzheimer's unit that you will encounter.

2. Specific Behaviors

There are a few specific behaviors you will encounter in a closed unit that may seem particularly odd. Alzheimer's sufferers who are able to walk by themselves often wander the hallways with agitated, determined pacing because they feel lost and disoriented or because they want to get away. Others wander aimlessly, for hours, probably because of damage to the brain, apparently disoriented in time and place. They may enter a room where you are visiting, say something incoherent, and leave as abruptly as they came. While this behavior may make us nervous, there is little cause for alarm. Even when people in later stages become very agitated, their anger is usually directed against caregivers who must make them do something they do not want to do. All you need do is "stay out of the way."

For example, if you see a woman walking around carrying one shoe, and she says she doesn't want to wear it, don't try to convince her otherwise. Should you observe a behavior that might result in harm, alert a staff person immediately. Do not physically intervene.

You may also encounter inappropriate sexual behavior, clinging or persistent following, repetitious actions, stubbornness and uncooperativeness, depression, apathy or listlessness. If any of these behaviors disturb you, the best you can do is ask for help or insight from the staff. If such behaviors make it difficult for you to visit with the person, again a staff person might be able to help you or at least explain to you what may be happening.

C. Responding

The picture we have painted may seem so bleak that you wonder if there is any hope of reaching Alzheimer's sufferers in any kind of effective ministry. Real contact, and thus real ministry—genuine pastoral visitation—is possible, but clearly we need to have in mind some new strategies—variations of what we normally use in pastoral visitation.

1. Learn from Staff

Professional staff who work in Alzheimer's units are, as we have indicated, specially trained for this work. Nurses' aides, housekeeping staff, and others who are in daily contact are also trained. These are people who are dealing with a variety of AD sufferers day in and day out. Usually they have developed a whole variety of skills and "tricks of the trade" that help them both manage behavior and establish authentic contact. We have met extraordinarily compassionate and gifted staff in these units who combine an ability to manage difficult behaviors competently with a profound certainty that the personhood of the AD sufferer is both intact and to be honored. We have also observed behavior on the part of staff that is less than exemplary. Staff, too, are human, and an Alzheimer's unit is not an easy place to work. Nonetheless, we can offer no better advice to a first-time visitor to one of these units than to ask for help and orientation (at a time negotiated with the staff). A first visit to an AD unit can be quite unnerving. Being with a person who is comfortable in that setting is reassuring and instructive.

2. The Self

A clear advantage for the staff is that they see people over time, day by day, and get to know them as persons. We who see these people infrequently are likely to be so distracted by the evidence of the disease (e.g. loss of speech, dramatic change in appearance, vacant stare, repetitious actions) that we respond to behaviors rather than to the person. People will say things like, "She's not who she used to be" or "He's just a shadow of his old self." We may nod in agreement. But the "core self"—the part of us that responds to our own name, the part we refer to when we say "I"—persists up to and into the last stage of the disease. The person will normally answer when you call that person by name; usually there is at least some clear recognition that you are speaking to "me." This implies that the person still possesses the essential self referred to in "I" statements. Twenty years ago I spoke with a neurologist about a friend in the early stages of dementia. I asked if it was Alzheimer's. I'll always remember his reply: "For his sake I hope not. Maybe he'll be lucky and it will be Pick's disease. At least with Pick's the highest centers of consciousness go first; with Alzheimer's they don't." Behaviors notwithstanding, the core self still exists.

Good news/bad news. Certainly we have to train ourselves to respond not to behaviors in Alzheimer's but to the person who suffers the disease. This is critical to ministry. The more we can help a person maintain a sense of self, and secondarily a sense of competence in doing what they can still do, the more real contact with the real person will be possible. As you watch skilled staff interact with AD sufferers, you will notice their care to challenge them to do as much as possible of what they previously did. They are helping the person maintain a sense not only of core identity but of secondary identities and competencies.

There is a story in the literature of a sufferer, Henry, who was introduced as follows: "This is Henry. Henry was a lawyer." Henry interrupted the proceedings by saying, "I *am* a lawyer." The point is that Henry maintained an awareness of the social identity that grew out of his profession. As far as he was concerned, though he was not practicing law, he remained a lawyer. Caregivers, including those of us in the ministry, can help to stem the erosion of these secondary selves by seeing the AD sufferer as a whole person, and responding thus. Time lovingly spent in attentive, loving presence or a shared pleasure is a precious gift.

3. The Family

Before we *finally* get to the visit, let us offer a word about your pastoral ministry with the family of the AD sufferer. As you can well imagine, they have very powerful feelings about their loved one: anger, embarrassment, helplessness, guilt, grief, worry, isolation—mixed, hopefully, with a sense of relief, realism, and Christian hope. Sometimes, especially with family members who don't visit regularly, there is denial of the seriousness of the disease or anger at the staff for "letting" their loved one get this way. As minister, you *will* get caught in the family's feelings. The best advice we have to offer is simply to hear them out, to focus on their feelings not your own ideas or convictions, and be supportive. There may be a time for prayer together; there may also be great anger against God that needs time to heal.

D. The Visit

1. Time

Just as with your initial visit to the nursing home, you may wish to contact the staff of the AD unit about the best time to visit. These units, while following the general routine of the rest of the facility, may have a rhythm of their own. Also, the person you are visiting may have a time of day when she tends to be more alert and less agitated. Some people suffering from AD try to sleep during the day because if they sleep at night and wake up in the dark, they feel disoriented and become frightened. Later, visiting on a set schedule may be especially helpful for people in these units, as patterned and repetitious behavior tends to be reassuring.

2. Dress

It may also be helpful to supply visual cues about who you are. Those who are ordained and who wear a clergy collar give a clear visual cue to their parishioner. For those who are not ordained, visual cues are not so easily given. Wearing a cross might be helpful, but an agitated, disoriented person could grab at the cross. Nevertheless, any visual cue that people might associate with the the church will help them to have some greater grasp of who you are and whom you represent.

3. Rituals

Because long-term memory remains longer than short-term memory, rituals (patterned behaviors) may evoke in Alzheimer's sufferers a sense of identify with or comfort in their tradition. I remember hearing of a woman, a German immigrant, who would frequently become combative. One day, as the woman was becoming difficult, a staff member began reciting the "Our Father" in German. The woman joined in, reciting along with her; she calmed down and became cooperative. Not all persons will have a "magic key" such as this. If they do, though, it is more than likely to be some "ritual" from their past that has significant religious or personal meaning for them. Examples include hymns familiar to all parishioners that resonate deeply with childhood memories. Other symbols are the cross, crucifix, altar, stole, oils, a bible or prayerbook, candles, blessed water, rosary beads, and so on. Equally important are prayers that are known from childhood. The celebration of mass and the giving of communion are rites to which even those whose memories have become empty or whose behavior is mildly disoriented may respond. The anointing of the sick might have a similar value if it was practiced in the home church or in the retirement home or nursing home before the onset of Alzheimer's disease.

Any of these "rituals" or patterned behaviors may resonate deeply in long-term memory and may bring the person some sense of personhood and of comfort in the presence of God. (Later in the book we devote a whole chapter to rituals.)

4. The Visit Itself

In your visit to the Alzheimer's unit, you will, at least at first, probably spend time only with your own parishioner. Later, you may have occasion to offer some time of prayer or worship for a larger group. Any visit should be prepared for by your own prayer, your focusing, your attention to the compassionate Christ. "Wherever two or three of you are gathered in my name..." can be very reassuring to the pastoral visitor.

Your individual pastoral visit can take the same shape as it would with a non-AD sufferer, with some modifications. You may wish to call the person by name, identify yourself, and add something like, "My name is _____, and I have come to visit you for a few minutes." How you proceed depends on the level or stage of the disease process and the kind of a day the person is having. *Greet the person.* It is critical to become present to the person—a word, a touch on the hand, whatever it takes for you to see past behaviors and greet the person as a person. *Speak the word.* We find it helpful to have something prepared to say—a familiar word from the scriptures, a few verses of a hymn, a prayer, a reassurance that although this is a hard time, "God still loves you and you matter to God." In the later stages of the disease this will be a one-way conversation although not necessarily a one-way communication. There will be times, even in the later stages of the disease, when there are glimmers of reaction that signal a response, however uncommunicable in words, to your presence. Sometimes, if appropriate, you may ask if the person would like to walk with you. If the facility has a chapel, a walk to it can be very good. *Share communion.* If sharing the eucharist is appropriate, it may evoke God's presence. However, depending on the condition of your parishioner, even eucharist may not be appropriate. Particularly with the agitated person, we have to find a way to touch into the long-term memory, to find a pathway to join a person's core self with the remembered consolation of God's presence. *Closure and blessing.* When you are ready to go (or when the person seems ready to have you go), you may end this as you would any pastoral visit with a blessing, the sign of the cross traced on the forehead, or a formal word of peace. On some occasions the person will cling to you; if appropriate, invite her to accompany you to the nurses' station where someone can help you leave gracefully.

If you have been visiting the facility for a while, you may wish to ask the activities director or a senior staff person about a worship service for anyone who would wish to attend. More of this later in the chapter on ritual.

All of this might seem like a lot of work. It can be. It might seem intimidating. It can be that too. But if we reach these people in their inner darkness and turmoil and bring them any amount of solace and comfort, we will have done God's work. If we don't seem to have accomplished anything, we can just commend the person to God and try again to reach her on our next visit. These mysteries cannot be approached—to paraphrase Thomas R. Cole—without humility and compassion, without acceptance of physical decline and mortality and a sense of the sacred.

E. The Dark Night of the Soul

At some point we will ask ourselves if there is anything within our religious tradition that allows us to speak in faith about this disease that seems to leave one's person so empty and dark. Without in any way celebrating the dimming of consciousness, I reflect that the conscious ego maybe a barrier rather than a path to God. In this I think of the words of John of the Cross, writing about the dark night of the soul. The parallels with AD and OBS are stunning; perhaps there is something here to help us look with more care, compassion, and even wonder at those who suffer.

> Wishing to strip them of this old [person] and clothe them with the new…God divests the faculties, affection, and sense, both spiritual and sensory, interior and exterior. He leaves the intellect in darkness, the will in aridity, the memory in emptiness, and the affections in supreme affliction, bitterness, and anguish, by depriving the soul of the feeling and satisfaction it pre-

viously obtained from spiritual blessing. For this privation is one of the conditions required that the spiritual form, which is the union of love, may be introduced into the spirit and united with it. The Lord works all this in the soul by means of a pure and dark contemplation ("The Dark Night," in *John of the Cross: Selected Writings*. Mahwah, NJ: Paulist Press, 1987, pp. 184-186).

5. Special Cases

*W*hat do you do when you have driven across town to the nursing home only to find that the person you planned to visit is asleep or otherwise indisposed? As much as possible, the determination of what to do should be made based on the realities of the individual you are visiting and his or her particular situation. But we can establish some common sense guidelines that we find helpful. In this chapter, we speak about several "special cases" that occur with some frequency in nursing home visitation: the person you are visiting is asleep, is sick, is moving into the late stages of a terminal illness, is unresponsive, or simply asks you to do a favor. We also consider a less-frequent case: when the person dies while you (and perhaps the family) are present.

A. The Person Is Asleep

If you arrive for a visit and your parishioner is asleep, you will have to decide whether or not to awaken the person. If you have not been visiting a person for any length of time, ask the nurses' aide who is taking care of your parishioner or the nurse who is in charge of the unit whether you should awaken him. The sleeping person may have been at physical therapy and be genuinely tired, or may be sick and need extra rest. In either of these cases the staff may recommend that you allow the person to sleep. But even this is not certain. For example, if you are visiting just prior to lunch or dinner the staff might want to wake the person for the visit so that he is awake and alert for mealtime. Staff will generally be glad to tell you whether the person should be or would want to be awakened. If you are visiting your parishioner with any regularity, the person will most likely have mentioned your visits to the staff and indicated his desires.

If you anticipate visiting a person over any length of time, ask the person after the first few visits what you should do in the event that you come and she is asleep. If the person you are visiting has a regular nap time, you need to know that in order to respect it. After all, we would not visit a parishioner at his home at 11 am if we knew that he works at night. We need to respect individual rhythms or needs even if we judge ourselves to be much busier people than those we are visiting. It may feel to you that a life in a nursing home is, practically speaking, of less importance (or, at least, urgency) than your busy life. On reflection, you may realize that this judgment does not respect the important tasks of life and growth, of love and responsibility, of an authentic moral career of the nursing home resident. To accord this as much importance as our own lives is sometimes a difficult leap of faith. In any case, visits can be negotiated. Empowering people you visit by respecting their input into the when and where of visiting will help to establish a better rapport.

B. The Person Is Sick

1. *Temporary Illness*

What if you arrive for the visit and the person is sick? Again, as much as possible, we must be sensitive to the individual's particular circumstances. Will the sickness prevent the person from being able to participate fully in the visit? Sometimes the answer is clear: e.g., a person suffering from diarrhea is not likely to want to receive visitors, especially if the person is of the opposite gender. Very likely, your parishioner will appreciate a few brief words of concern and an offer to come back another time. Sometimes the answer is less clear: the sickness may be temporary (a flu, a cold, an attack of arthritis, etc.) and this may or may not impair the person's ability to participate in the visit. This depends in part on your abilities, style, and the purpose of the visit.

2. Preparing for Visitation in Time of Terminal Illness

In this section, the special case we focus on is pastoral visitation with someone who is beginning to show signs of becoming severely debilitated or terminally ill. Specifically, we will consider preparation with the sick person for your visitations and ministry when the person is too ill or too weak to make her wishes known. What you can offer as options will vary based on your tradition and theirs. But it will be best to discuss in advance what parishioners will expect of you when they are too weak or ill to tell you. This will make your work a little easier later on, will make their hard experiences (hopefully) more tolerable, and will make the comfort and consolation of the scriptures more immediate. In the very late stages of a terminal illness the visit may become very one-sided. At that point, your intentional preparation will make a great difference in the quality of your pastoral care and in your personal comfort level.

When visiting with a person in the earlier stages of a terminal illness, discuss with her your mutual plans for her spiritual care late in the illness. Some of us—most of us, probably—find this difficult, even ghoulish. Isn't it better to talk about something more cheerful? An emphatic "No!" In most cases, it is we who are afraid to broach the subject of death, not the person who is approaching death—this "birth-ordained reality." The alternative to this kind of frank conversation is ministry that is less effective and inevitably less personal.

If you know a person's favorite bible passages in advance, this knowledge will relieve you of the anxiety of trying to pick something you think appropriate. If a parishioner has favorite prayers, or a favored style of prayer, these are going to be more comforting and meaningful to her in a time of (possible) physical distress than something she has never heard before. Besides the sacramental rites of the church, there are many books that include outlines of services for the sick, with suggested scripture readings and prayers. These may be used as presented or as guidelines. Inevitably, some of this will be unfamiliar to older congregants. This argues all the more so for preparation. While these services might have some merit for one who has never been exposed to them, we contend that they will be far more comforting to the sufferer if they have been presented, explained, put in context, and agreed on before their use becomes necessary. Once again, the more preparation you can do for this time, the more helpful it will be to both of you. The very act of preparation will be a good ministry and will give the person an opportunity to speak openly about fears and wishes, and both opportunity and impetus to set things right if necessary.

3. *Visitation with a Very Ill Person*

In this section we address the issue of visitation with a parishioner who is very ill, with whom you have not had time to prepare properly for ministry in this circumstance. If you find yourself in this situation, take a moment to let go of any guilt for your lack of preparedness (it will only interfere with your ministry). Then, using the type of four-step visit we discussed earlier, minister to this person as a sister or brother in Christ. The steps or phases of the visit can be adjusted in length and content to make them appropriate to

the person you are visiting and your knowledge of and relationship with her. The assumption in this is that the person
you are visiting is extremely ill and very limited in ability to
respond.

An aside: the first time or first few times you find yourself in an apparently one-sided situation with a parishioner,
you may feel *very awkward*. Indeed, you may find yourself
looking over your shoulder to be sure no one hears you
talking to this apparently unresponsive person. This may
be less an issue when the person is newly ill; it certainly
will be more an issue when the person has been unresponsive for a long time. Don't lose courage: hearing may per-
sist even when the ability to respond externally is gone. If
that is the case, your presence and ministry may be extraordinarily helpful, although you will never know for certain.

Let's assume that the person you are visiting is someone
you do not know well, someone with whom you have not
discussed how you will minister when the person is very
limited in ability to respond. How then will our visit differ
from the four-step visit we proposed earlier?

(a) *Greeting the Person.* This phase of the visit is intended
to bring the person you are visiting into your presence, in a
spirit of attention, compassion, and faith in the presence of
Christ in your midst. The barriers to presence in this situation are quite specific. Lack of response is the first and most
obvious. We have learned since childhood to "back off" if
the person we greet "ignores" our greeting. We can over-
come this by attention to our faith that together we stand in
the loving presence of God. The second barrier is a little
more subtle, namely the ability of a disease or physical condition to define how we see a person. We need to be intentional not to treat the person as his disease. We may have
heard that this is sometimes a problem for physicians, but it
can easily be a problem for us as well. Part of our preparation for our visit can be reminding ourselves that Mr. Jones

is more than a cancer patient; he is a person who *has* a sickness called cancer. In the actual visit, we may get past this
barrier to presence by being consistent in our approach. If
we normally would hold a parishioner's hand or lay our
hand on his arm or shoulder, do so now. Relax; be in touch
with your own feelings (positive and negative). When you
yourself know you are present to this person (whatever the
response or lack of response) you are ready to move on.

(b) *Speaking the Word.* This phase of the visit is intended to
bring to the person a word that connects the person to the
Word of God as that Word illumines, comforts, uplifts, for-
gives, sustains. Again, we remind you that the sick person's
ability to hear and ability to respond are not the same. Speak
slowly, speak articulately, speak loudly enough to be heard.
Assuming that you have not discussed favorite scriptures
with the person and have no prior knowledge of what this
person might like, it is up to you to choose scriptures that
are, in your judgment, appropriate. The "Magnificat," the
"Prayer of Simeon," the "Our Father," selections from the
passion narratives, the resurrection accounts, the disciples
on the road to Emmaus—these are but a few possible choices. You might also want to consider, after the scriptures, the
Gloria, the doxology, the "Our Father"—any familiar liturgical texts. Such prayers can be an integral part of bringing
to this person the consolation of God's word.

(c) *Sharing Communion.* The goal of this step of the visit is
to help the person come to a moment of depth, or intensity,
or intimacy with God. This may feel like the most difficult
step in such a visit because this visit is largely, if not exclusively, one-sided and because there is little prior ground-
work or relationship. Yet, this moment of communion is not
exclusively dependent on our resources or our previous
relationship. You might consider acutally giving the person
holy communion, if in the judgment of the nursing staff
your parishioner has an appropriate level of awareness.

If communion is not permitted for health reasons (the person may have difficulty swallowing, for example) or appropriate because of the level of awareness, prayer may help the person come to an awareness of depth of communion or intimacy with God. If at all possible, your prayer should be prepared in advance. While impromptu prayers may seem more sincere, the effort put into preparation will be reflected in carefully chosen words that convey to the person that she matters to God and that God cares for her. A prepared prayer may also bring the person into an awareness of being in the body of Christ by reminding her that she is in the thoughts and prayers of her congregation. Even if the person cannot join you, ending your prayer with the "Our Father" may communicate to the person that she is still part of the believing community that supports her in prayer.

(d) *Blessing and Closure.* The purpose of this phase of the visit is more than a formalized goodbye. It is a blessing and a commendation of this person to God in the course of this arduous spiritual task. In this particular situation, both elements are important: the blessing, because of its healing power; the commendation to God's mercy, because you are leaving the person to face—with God's help—difficult hours and days. Once again, your own clarity about the person's spiritual needs can give intensity and focus to your words. You leave a brother in Christ to face final demands, perhaps prolonged suffering, perhaps death.

You may feel a certain relief that the visit is over. Or you may feel a certain guilt about leaving the person and question whether you have "accomplished" anything. Yet, the visit must end. A blessing, preferably with a laying on of the hands, and a few personal words make effective closure.

C. The Person Is Unresponsive

1. Unresponsiveness Because of Anger, Anxiety, Loss, etc.

In this section we consider appropriate ministry when we find a person unresponsive either because of anger, anxiety, loss, etc. or because of abuse. By unresponsive we mean that a person refuses to speak, is deeply lethargic, is in a coma, or seems to be in "another place."

If a previously responsive person fails to respond to you when you come to visit, find out through consultation with the staff the reason for this change. There may be an organic reason (reversible or irreversible) for the person's condition. If there is an organic cause, then we suggest conducting the visit in the way we discussed above. Current medical opinion holds that hearing is the last sensory function lost (if the person's hearing has been normal all along) for a person who is in a coma or unresponsive. Thus, even if a person gives no indication of being aware of your presence, use of familiar scriptures, prayers, etc. can still reach him and may be appreciated more than we will ever know. Some also suggest giving communion to unresponsive people if communion has been a part of our prior ministry to them. Of course, in this case, staff should be consulted about the medical appropriateness of communion—the wafer or wine could induce choking.

If the staff indicates no organic cause for the lack of responsiveness, inquire of the staff if there are other reasons. If no one is able to give a reason, you yourself may try to determine a cause. This may strike you as odd: surely it is not your business to try to find out why a person is unresponsive. Actually, though, it may be. We recommend that you take a little time to assess the cause of the unresponsiveness. Its cause may well demand your attention—anger, anxiety, a sense of abandonment, old angers, even abuse—in particular if no one else is attending to it.

In an institutional environment, a variety of conditions may trigger unresponsiveness. For example, a person may feel anger and anxiety over perceived abandonment by the family in admission to the nursing home. Losses may have occurred in the person's immediate family or circle of friends. Physical losses (sight, mobility, etc.) may have been recently suffered. Old angers may have surfaced, triggered by some recent communication or event. Or there may be new angers that feel unsafe or dangerous to express in this nursing home environment. In any of these cases, the person may withdraw into unresponsiveness.

Our hope is that if you name the problem in a general way, the person will respond—perhaps verbally, perhaps only in body-language—in some way that opens communication. For example, "You seem very sad and quiet today. Something must be wrong, because you are usually glad to speak with me. Perhaps you are angry, or something bad has happened to you...." If after several attempts the person does not speak, you may wish to say, "I'd like to be able to help but I can't unless you let me. I'll think about you during the week and come by again next week. Let me say a prayer with you and ask God's blessing."

If on a second round you find you are not getting anywhere, and if your conversation with staff yields no organic or behavioral clues, you may want to pursue the matter further with staff and/or family, and encourage a consultation with a psychologist. It is a terrible thing to be reduced to silence (or to reduce oneself to silence). Another professional might be able to help the person out of this prison even though we were not able to.

2. *Unresponsiveness Because of Abuse*

Finally, withdrawal might also be a result of abuse by the staff—perceived or real. Unfortunately, real abuse does continue to occur in nursing homes. Even the best facilities are not immune to the potential for abuse. Often, low paid workers bring their own angers and frustrations to work with them and strike out, verbally or physically, at residents they believe are being difficult. Compounding the problem is the feeling among many residents in institutional care that if they complain and are not believed or the employee is not removed, they will be vulnerable to retaliation by the employee or marked as a troublemaker by staff. Even where staff take allegations of resident abuse seriously, these fears can be very unnerving. If abuse is indicated, you need to report it to the appropriate staff—a charge nurse or administrator. (In an extreme case, where conversation with head staff does not change a pattern of abuse, you may even have to contact the local or state long-term care ombudsman or even Adult Protective Services. This will be rare. We ourselves have never run across such a case.) The ombudsman is an individual appointed to investigate complaints about nursing homes, and the ombudsman's phone number should be posted in every nursing home. Adult Protective Services is a state agency that is charged with the protection of threatened or injured adults.

D. Requests for Favors

A less serious problem, but one requiring sensitivity and common sense, is responding to a parishioner's request for a favor. A few examples will give you an idea of what might happen. For example, a parishioner might complain that his family doesn't visit, and ask you to call and tell them they ought to visit. If indeed you know that this is the case, the request might well fall within your scope of responsibilities. However, the family may actually visit once a week and your parishioner may not think that is enough or may simply not remember the visits. Sorting this out gracefully takes, as we have said, sensitivity and common sense.

Sometimes your response is clearer. For example, the request may be potentially harmful. If a person asks you to bring her candy or some type of food, first check with the medical staff to determine if it is consistent with any dietary restrictions the person may have. Even if the staff says it is OK, you have to decide if you want to start this pattern of behavior. If the person does not receive many visits, she may begin to see you as an errand runner. While every person must be treated with generosity, there are con artists among the elderly in nursing homes—just as there are truly desperate people. If a person has a legitimate need but you do not feel you have adequate time, you might seek out some volunteers from your congregation to try to meet the need.

Where the request clearly contravenes the institution's rules, your obligations are clear. For example, smokers' cigarettes are kept at the nurses' desk so that people don't try to smoke in restricted areas. However heartfelt a request to bring cigarettes to an individual's room, this would never be appropriate. Some other requests are not going to be so easy to assess. For example, a person might ask your help in changing a will. You may judge that this falls within your pastoral responsibility after you have explored with the person the reason for the request. You may decide that you should not act: someone might be trying to con the person into something and you would be an unwitting accomplice. Examples of other requests that take careful weighing include a request to call friends or relatives or take a message to someone. You have to assess each of these cases individually and decide what is an appropriate response in the context of the pastor-parishioner relationship.

E. The Death of a Resident

A final special case occurs when you are present at the death of a parishioner. We assume that your usual pastoral skills will serve you well in this case. We do make suggestions specific to the nursing home. First, whether the family is present or not, it is very important to go out into the hallway and invite nearby staff to join you in prayer around the bedside of the person who has just died. Staff have taken care of this person day in and day out, perhaps for years. Many have formed deep attachments. Many have a strong sense of faith that can support the family (and you). Often the staff can console the family in ways that you cannot. For their part, this invitation honors the care they give and honors their relationship to the parishioner who has died.

Second, staff bear a particular burden with each death, namely the accumulation of grief because there is little time or opportunity to process their sorrow. A friend told me recently that she had started each day's nursing shift for the past week with the death of a resident of whom she had become very fond. For each she could only say a quick prayer and then move on to care for the living. When grief is left unacknowledged and deaths are left unmourned there can be a build-up of anger or depression.

Some of the staff may have mixed emotions on the death of a resident. While people may *say*, "It's best that she died; it's a blessing and a mercy," there may be, along with a genuine sense of relief, enormous sorrow, pent-up guilt, anger, etc. Careful listening and focused attention are invaluable in sorting out what is going on and responding appropriately. There may be little formal opportunity for this. Perhaps the best that can happen in some circumstances is that you are so deeply aware of what is unspoken that you can communicate a presence and a compassion that heals the healers.

Whatever is said about the staff with the death of a resident can also be applied to other residents. Those who die have been important in the lives of people, there in the nursing home where they live. Sometimes of course a death seems merciful. But often there is, whatever the age of the person who dies, a real empty place left in many hearts. We think of Vernon Satterwaite who, until the week he died, pulled himself around in his wheelchair, cheering up everyone he met. Vernon was one hundred and two years old. He is greatly missed. We think of those whose roommate of many years dies, and who have the burden of starting over. Ruth Howard Gray, in her late eighties, writes simply and poignantly from a retirement home about a dear friend. "Mr. Brown is dead. He died Thursday at 7 am. His death was rather sudden. [...] Yes, he would have wanted to go quickly. But the fact remains, he is gone. [...] The suddenness of it is like a whiplash to me" (*Survival of the Spirit: My Detour Through a Retirement Home*. Atlanta: John Knox, 1985, pp. 82, 84).

With the apostle Paul we affirm that whether we live or whether we die we are the Lord's. Yet neither this affirmation of faith nor our sense that death may seem more "normal" in a nursing home setting should diminish the seriousness and compassion of our response.

6. Sacraments and Rituals

*I*n this chapter we address more fully the celebration of sacraments and rituals in a nursing home setting. We explore some dynamics of baptism and eucharist, and then discuss how the celebration of these sacraments and of rituals may bring participants into the experience of God's love, may bond them in communion, may heal and console. Our discussion attends to four distinct groups: responsive nursing home residents, the frail old, the unresponsive, and confused nursing home residents. As we go along, we will comment on the why of rituals as well as the what. At the end, we add a brief note on creating your own rituals.

A. Baptism and Communion

In this section, we reflect on the experience of baptism and eucharist, and then inquire about the nature and function of ritual. Our purpose is twofold: first, to explore sacraments that are on-going realities in the lives of nursing home residents; second, to reflect on the nature and importance of rituals.

1. Reflection on Experience

Baptism and eucharist are defining moments in the Christian life. Their power lies in their link to Christ in the witness of the New Testament; their power lies in the witness of faith of the community that celebrates them; their power lies in the wholeness of the act of washing or going down into the waters of baptism, there to die and rise with Christ; their power lies in the wholeness of a simple sharing of bread and wine; their power lies in communal celebration; their power lies in doing a graceful act. Words and actions connect us to the world of Peter and Paul, to the worlds of Mary and Julian of Norwich, to the worlds of Francis and Clare, to the worlds of Calvin and Luther, to the worlds of Mother Teresa and Martin Luther King, Jr., to the worlds of our grandparents and parents and all those who have been our ancestors in the faith. The connection is more profound than words alone can express. Actions and words—the stuff of ritual and sacrament—help bring us into the presence of the mystery. Of eucharist, Eugene Peterson writes in *Under the Unpredictable Plant: An Exploration in Vocational Holiness* (Grand Rapids, MI: Eerdmans):

> Eucharist is not as much interested in using words to define meaning as to deepen mystery, to enter into the ambiguities, push past the safely known into the risky unknown. The Christian Eucharist uses the simplest of words—this is my body, this is my blood—to plunge us into the depths of love, to venture into what is not tied down, into love, into faith. These words do not describe; they reveal, they point, they reach.

Reflection on experience tells us that the great events of our life in Christ are shaped and expressed by the words and rituals of sacraments. Such is the case for us; it is also the case for those with whom we minister in the nursing home.

2. The Nature and Function of Ritual: Being in Communion

What happens in ritual (whether it be baptism, or the folding of the flag, or a formal Sunday dinner)? Rituals involve doing; we don't just *talk about* baptism—we baptize.

Rituals are repetitive—and by their repetitive character provide a message of pattern and predictability in places of uncertainty, worry, or impotence. Rituals dramatize—we act out our beliefs elaborately so that they become vivid and trustworthy. Rituals connect us—to ourselves, to past and future, to wider groups not-now-present, to an order that quiets and sustains. Rituals bring genuine sharing and bonding; they act out our common commitments and promises.

If these claims seem too large, think of important rituals that shape our lives with all their symbolic acting-out of hoped-for realities—birthdays, weddings, funerals, reunions, family gatherings, holding a new-born for the first time, or even the simpler rituals of daily life. All strong rituals bring us somehow into profound communion—the whole of us, body, spirit, mind, ancestors and those yet unborn—with ourselves and with each other. This is of particular importance in relationship to the nursing home, where disconnectedness, loneliness, and silence are ever-present dangers.

B. Rituals in the Nursing Home

Various denominations have much in common in sacraments and use of ritual, although actual practices vary substantially. As pastoral ministers, we will respect the tradition our parishioners come from. At the same time, we may explore richer ways of using rituals for people whose lives now need more than ever the reassurance that sacraments and rituals can afford them. In this section, then, we will work through a variety of rituals that may be used in the nursing home (the list is not exhaustive), referring to four groups: the responsive nursing home resident, the frail (or "old") nursing home resident, the unresponsive nursing home resident, and the confused nursing home resident.

1. *The Responsive Nursing Home Resident*

A. BAPTISM

The celebration of baptism in the nursing home may be rare. We mention it here, though, for three reasons. First, it may be that your ministry or that of the staff and other residents helps an unbaptized person in the nursing home come to faith in Jesus Christ, and so seek baptism. It would not be right to exclude this as a possibility. Age is not an impossible barrier to God's grace! Keeping this open as an option may widen our sense of ministry and our outreach in the nursing home. Second, we invite consideration of the baptism in the nursing home of a child of the church where a grandparent lives. Although clearly an exception to common practice, it would be a wonderful witness to faith and a powerful expression of commitment to bring a small group of family and other parishioners to the nursing home to perform an infant grandchild's baptism there. Third, we recommend the reaffirmation of baptismal vows in liturgical or prayer settings. Exactly how this is worked out will vary according to circumstances and season of the liturgical year. The key element is an invitation to remember our baptism into Christ (this may be done formally, using a series of questions, or informally, in the telling of stories), to celebrate lives lived in the church, and to restate our commitment to Christ and our reliance on salvation through his cross and resurrection. The ritual use of water (*not* rebaptism, of course, but neither simply a perfunctory sprinkling) may evoke more powerfully our connection and communion.

B. EUCHARIST

This most commonly celebrated sacrament is a powerful way of helping people be reincorporated into the body of

Christ and be strengthened by God's presence. Even the common name for eucharist, namely "communion," suggests what this sacrament can help bring about: sharing, bonding, sacrificial involvement with one another, union with Christ. For those who can no longer go out to church, restriction to the nursing home often signals the end of celebration of the eucharist. Yet our parishioners have a right to share in the body of Christ in this sacrament. *How* eucharist is shared in the nursing home, the physical condition of responsive residents, the physical space in which we can celebrate, and the ordained or non-ordained status of the pastoral visitor will also give shape to our celebration of eucharist or communion. Where possible, all the rituals of eucharist should be observed. The familiar is part of what brings a sense of connectedness. As much as possible, we want to utilize all the senses to reach out to this person to let them know that they are being included in the worship of the church. Thus, simply "giving communion" will, all things being equal, have a lesser effect in bringing a person to a sense of being "in communion" than the celebration of the whole rite of communion or a full celebration of eucharist.

C. CELEBRATIONS OF FRIENDSHIP AND COMMITMENT

Weddings in nursing homes and long-term care facilities are not unheard of, although they may be relatively unusual. Should you have the good fortune to counsel with people preparing to marry, and the joy of actually celebrating the marriage with them, you may find the experience an extraordinary revelation of the humanness of the old. More likely, though, you will celebrate anniversaries of weddings, whether the partner is alive or not. We think it is a lovely, gracious way of ministering to celebrate and give thanks for years of life lived together. Why should the resident have no one to help her bring to mind and give thanks for her married life? How this actually works out will require your pastoral ingenuity, but within the context of a worship service there may be an opportunity to speak about, remember, grieve, and celebrate. I think of a friend whose husband died quite young. On the first anniversary of his death she was surrounded by people who cared deeply for her; on the second anniversary—when her memories were strong and her sorrow real—no one remembered.

In a similar vein, we recommend celebrating new friendships and commitments in the nursing home, resident/resident and resident/staff. Even in bad times, people do care for and look out for each other; people are committed to each other; people practice "random acts of kindness." Would it not be wonderful to celebrate this ritually in the context of worship and thanksgiving?

D. ANOINTING OF THE SICK

While the anointing of the sick may be familiar to some parishioners in the nursing home, others may only remember this sacrament as "extreme unction" and may associate it with closeness to death. Where the anointing of the sick is familiar, it can be a powerful source of consolation, awareness of forgiveness, and inner healing. What about its use for those residents who only remember extreme unction, or who do not know either rite?

Our advice? Talk it over with your parishioner in advance; make it celebrative; let this be a vehicle of presence and prayer. These services of healing have been carefully worked out; they are rich in their scripture readings and prayers. For people in a nursing home who are daily rubbed and massaged with lotion, a simple anointing on the forehead and hands with oil in the sign of the cross can hardly be intrusive. Signing with oil or the laying on of hands can communicate a powerful message of communion and connectedness.

E. LIVING LITURGICAL TIME

As a parish minister visiting in a nursing home, you may not have much opportunity to influence the overall shape of the daily and weekly schedule. Nonetheless, you may be able to help responsive residents to be more attentive to the seasons of the liturgical year. At two Jewish nursing homes we know (in each there is a full-time rabbi), the week and the seasons are organized from sabbath to sabbath, from holy day to holy day. A Jewish woman said, "When I make the movement, circling the sabbath candles, calling their holiness to me, covering my eyes, then I feel my mother's hands on my smooth cheeks" (Barbara Myerhoff, op. cit., p. 327). Surely this body-memory is preferable to marking time by Oprah, Phil, and Geraldo! Even on a small scale, helping your parishioners be attentive to the seasons of the year—Lent, Easter, Pentecost, Ordinary Time, Advent, Christmas, Epiphany—may provide a more healthy structure for living and a more creative approach to time. Here *chronos* (raw time) becomes *kairos* (the moment of grace). Each season admits of rituals and symbols, of prayers and memories. We are fairly good at bringing Christmas symbols and rituals into the nursing home (although so is everyone else). Perhaps we can be more attentive to Lent (for people who are in some measure living the way of the cross), to Easter (for people who must live in the hope of God's saving power), to Pentecost (for people who need God's enlivening Spirit), to Ordinary Time (for people who know ordinariness too well), to Advent (for those who wait). Personally we may have some discomfort with or resistance to ritualizing the liturgical year. We doubt if our congregants will share our squeamishness. On the contrary, experience tells us there can be rich and helpful symbols and rituals of these "seasons" that accomplish two important tasks. They ease our preparation for visitation; they provide powerful signs of communion, connection, and meaning.

F. RITES OF CONNECTION TO CHURCH

At a church we know, lay ministers who take communion to the sick and shut-in refer to their tasks as threefold: God, gospel, and *gossip*! The point is important. Life in the church also includes being in touch with the lives, stories, and happenings of those with whom we share communion. Sharing parish bulletins, announcements, stories of "goings-on" at the church, banners, photos of youth groups or parish gatherings—these are all rites of connection to the church. They are important signs of communion. Besides, they are fun and easy to share. On their own, they may even structure a very creative pastoral visit.

In a slightly different key, saying the rosary, watching mass on TV, listening to a tape-recorded Sunday celebration or to tapes of sacred music (old or contemporary) can function as power ways of connection to church. At a very practical level, it may be important for some parishioners that someone provide the tape-recorder or stay to help in managing it.

G. RITES OF PASSAGE

Passage *into* the nursing home is such a potentially traumatic event that we have focused on this in the following chapter. But there are many passages in the life of a nursing home resident that could be ritualized. This requires innovation. Barbara Myerhoff notes that in between retirements and funerals "there is a universe of differentiation that remains a cultural wasteland for each to calculate and navigate alone, without the aid of ritual, ceremony, or symbol" (ibid., p. 312). Even in a very large sense, passage from assisted living to health care, acceptance of a walker or wheelchair, acceptance of a roommate, and the death of another resident are passages that may, in being ritualized, become more bearable.

2. The Frail Old (the "Old-Old")

Much of what has already been said applies to the frail old. In this section we spell out some differences.

A. INABILITY TO ATTEND OR DEAL WITH PUBLIC WORSHIP

Many of the frail old, although not confused, have trouble focusing their attention long enough to fully participate in corporate worship for physical reasons (discomfort sitting in one position for any length of time, medications that affect the ability to concentrate). General discomfort from physical problems produced by very old age can cause these folks to avoid corporate worship altogether. Sometimes the reasons are emotional or mental. These parishioners require special attention, often in small group or individual prayer times and in rituals. In the section that follows, we note some differences that may occur because of physical frailty. In the next section we pay attention to rituals for those who are unresponsive or confused.

B. VARIATIONS ON RITUALS ALREADY DISCUSSED

Most of what has already been said can be relatively easily modified to suit the needs of the frail old (some of whom will be bed-ridden). Four issues seem worth mentioning. The first is the need, whenever possible, to gather people into small groups. Most rituals that connect will be more effective if there is some congregation, however small. The second is the need to respect the physical limitations of the frail old. Usually a simple question about how they are doing will elicit the information we need to adapt our ministry and reshape the ritual (whether that be eucharist, a rite of healing such as anointing of the sick or a less formal ritual, a rite of passage, a renewal of baptism, etc.). Third, there may be specific rituals that are of importance to those who are among the frail old. In particular, we refer you back to the section on preparation for pastoral visitation when people are no longer able to respond verbally. Lastly, a word to the pastoral minister: This can be very labor-intensive work. Whatever its intrinsic value, you will find yourself weighing how much time you can spend with individuals and small groups. (This will be even more so in the case of the unresponsive person.) There is both reward and discipline in this kind of ministry. Be gentle with yourself.

3. *The Unresponsive Nursing Home Resident*

We have already spoken about visiting unresponsive residents (in Chapter 5). In this section, we concentrate on connecting with them through sacrament and ritual. For the confused and the unresponsive individual, periods of contact are less common than with the responsive. Contact or communion is a great gift to the individual who may be struggling against encroaching confusion. Contact with the confused and unresponsive through religious ritual helps create for them a sanctuary in their inner loneliness. Words or actions associated with early experiences of life in the church may be a reminder of God's love. There are reasons to believe that what we do reaches these parishioners so that, in their own way, they are able to respond to God's presence and find some solace in it. Long-term memory outlasts short-term memory. "Conceivably, any kind of ritual has the capacity to retrieve a fragment of past life. Rituals associated with and originating in childhood are more likely to do so [...]. Two characteristics of these rituals are salient here: first, their intensely physiological associations, and, second, their great power and immediacy, coming as they do from the individual's first emotional social experiences" (ibid., p. 327).

We may find this kind of ministry disconcerting because we see so little response. Two anecdotes from the perspective of nursing home professionals may alleviate our discomfort. On one occasion, with some trepidation, I asked a social worker for the names of four unresponsive residents who might (based on what she knew of their past) want to receive communion. Somewhat to my surprise, she answered enthusiastically. She had much clearer convictions than I did about the good this could do. In another facility, a chaplain tells us that when she brings communion to now-unresponsive individuals she sees changes in facial features that indicate to her some sense of recognition. We trust her experience and judgment.

When we celebrate eucharist in a formal way with a group of the somewhat-unresponsive, our words ought to be brief and focused. Our attention should be on ritual actions and familiar prayers and texts associated with celebrating eucharist. Our actions should be "larger" (but not over-exaggerated) than they might normally be. Make sure the person can see you prepare the bread and pour the wine. At the time for communion, bring the elements to each individual as you say "The body of Christ" and "The blood of Christ." Be prepared for some awkwardness, and perhaps for some jerkiness of movement. Above all, be prepared for your own less-than-perfectly-skilled reactions.

When unresponsive persons are bedridden, we must, of course, bring communion *to them*. As we become more familiar with individuals, our practice will become more skilled. The four-step framework we proposed earlier provides a starting-point. *Greet the person.* We simply go to the person's room, knock and enter. We greet her by name, tell her that we have come to bring her communion, and take a moment to become present to her. *Speak the word.* Our words can be very brief and focused. Any familiar psalm, liturgical text, or prayer may serve to awaken a memory or awareness, however dim, of God's loving presence. *Share communion.* Using the appropriate words, break a very small piece of communion bread and place it in her mouth.

Depending on the state of the person, we may use a dropper or syringe (the kind used to give liquids to unresponsive people) to give her the consecrated wine. Sometimes it is easiest to dip the communion bread into the consecrated wine and then place it in her mouth, or simply share the communion bread only, which is the common experience for many older parishioners. *Blessing.* With your hand on her head or shoulder, say a blessing or final prayer, and then leave, commending this person in your heart to God's compassion.

4. The Confused Nursing Home Resident

Sometimes we bring eucharist to people who are confused. This can be disconcerting to the pastoral minister. A few guidelines might alleviate some anxiety. If a person becomes overly agitated, stop what you are doing for a moment. If the agitation continues or starts up again when you continue, simply stop as gracefully as you can. After your visit, talk with staff and family about the situation. There may be individuals with whom you will not be able to work or times when a particular form of ministry is not suitable.

When a confused person responds *verbally* in an inappropriate way (without becoming agitated) you may carry on. If the response is *an action* you cannot ignore (e.g., a person begins to undress), stop and address the behavior with the person in a firm but gentle manner. If the behavior continues and is so disconcerting that you cannot continue, stop what you are doing and try gracefully to end the visit, without just walking out. Later in conversation with the nursing staff or social worker you may get some insight into the cause of the behavior and some strategies that help you minister more effectively.

C. Creating Rituals

Sometimes you may want to create your own rituals. By all means experiment. Worship in the nursing home can be a wonderful laboratory for our growth as pastoral ministers. Here are a few guidelines. First, emphasize simplicity. For either confused or unresponsive patients, lengthy and elaborate ceremony will be unproductive; it may even have an adverse effect on the confused elderly. Second, in choosing what you will try, be attentive to your own gifts and limitations. For example, if you are comfortable singing alone, *a capella*, sing a familiar hymn in the ritual you create. Third, pay attention to detail, coordinating words and actions. For those who have learned to sign for the deaf, simple signing or "acting out" of the words of a song may help communicate its meaning. Lastly, try to involve as many of the senses as possible. For example, smell is a powerful memory trigger. Incense, or other scents that are associated with worship such as pine boughs at Christmas, may be helpful.

As you have read through this chapter, it has no doubt struck home just how much is asked of you as pastoral minister in a nursing home. All through this chapter, your pastoral creativity has been challenged. In this context as in so many other difficult ministry contexts, we count on God's grace and move on one step at a time. We do what we can to bring God's comfort to those who suffer and leave the rest to the Holy Spirit.

7. Leaving Home, Entering the Nursing Home

*A*s we noted in the Introduction, we have left this discussion of entrance into the nursing home until you, the pastoral visitor, are comfortable with and knowledgeable about nursing homes. Visiting extensively in nursing homes can give you a most helpful perspective from which to speak with the person facing entrance into a nursing home

The moment of entrance into a nursing home is extraordinarily traumatic for most new residents and for their families. To this point, we have taken the perspective of the pastoral visitor. In the first part of this chapter, we shift our perspective to that of the nursing home resident. We look at the specifics of the experience of leaving home and entering a nursing home and discuss the feelings and tasks faced by the new resident. Only then do we consider the role of the pastoral minister. We make suggestions for the pastoral minister before the parishioner enters the nursing home and discuss the pastoral minister's role in the actual transition, with the new resident, the family, and the congregation. Finally, we speak of the mutual engagement of congregation and nursing home resident in ministry.

Given the scope of this book, why focus on this specific moment, albeit a traumatic moment, in the life of a nursing home resident? First, this transition has such specific dynamics that it warrants special attention. Second, this transition lets us see some of the emotional and spiritual struggles the new nursing home resident undergoes—and prevails over. In *The Measure of My Days* (New York: Penguin, 1968, p. 5), Florida Scott-Maxwell writes that if age "is a long defeat it is also a victory, meaningful for the initiates of the time, if not for those who have come less far. [...] Age is truly a time of heroic helplessness."

A. Leaving Home

For the first time in the history of the world, the old now anticipate death by degenerative rather than infectious disease. The prayer of the Roman liturgy, "From a sudden and unprovided for death protect us" begins to be balanced by Robert Blythe's elegant phrase, "This then is her quandary: the slow-motion departure" (*The View in Winter*. New York: Penguin, 1979, p. 10). Unless they, like the one-horse carriage, fall apart completely in one moment of one day, they must anticipate possible entrance into a long-term care facility.

For many of those who are now old, this is a dreaded thought. Many have memories of the "poor house" that color present perceptions; more have experiences of visiting in places they were only too happy to leave. The impact of entrance into the nursing home can be viewed from two perspectives: what is being left and what is being faced. In this section we look at entrance into the nursing home from both perspectives, explore the emotional impact (anger, uselessness, loneliness), and discuss the tasks of reorganization and adaptation.

1. Impact of Leaving Home

Most people put a very personal imprint on the place where they live. (With the generation that is entering long-term care, home is often a single-family dwelling.) Self-constituting memories get put into the walls and fabric of the house. Over the years, people collect their "treasures"; things are arranged in certain ways so that are comfortable. People's furniture becomes them (in both senses); even the old scuffs and marks are familiar parts of the home-scape. Home is a place to live out a rhythm of life—cooking and eating, talking and resting, sharing struggles and love. To leave home is to leave an embodied expression of the self.

Most people face "leaving home" several times: leaving to go to school, leaving one place to move to another, seeing a grandparents' home put up for sale. In most of these cases there is a sense of timeliness and deliberateness—even choice. For the nursing home resident, departure from the home is sometimes sudden and traumatic—an illness which has required hospitalization leaves the person too weak to return home; the person is brought by ambulance to a long-term care facility. Where Medicare or Medicaid is involved, there is not even a choice of location—the first available bed becomes one's lot in life and death. Even when the departure is not sudden, it is characteristically unprepared for: the movers arrive at seven in the morning, and the home (the self) is dismantled with little chance to grieve the loss and to say goodbye. This particular form of unpreparedness is not necessary, although it happens all too often. (A useful resource for saving memories of home in a healthy manner is: *Memories of Home* by R. Best and J. Brunner. Mahwah, NJ: Paulist, 1994.)

When people leave their homes there are other familiar parts of the home landscape that are lost: neighbors, stores, places to walk—all small but real parts of the self. There may also be the loss of a parish church where a person has worshiped and prayed for many years. Although it may strike us as odd, one feature of a familiar place of worship is that you don't have to do much work to pray. Once you arrive, there is something that takes you up, there is something that supports you in worship: familiar people who turn with you in quiet attention to God; familiar voices and hymns; the rhythm of the celebration of the eucharist; the voices of children and older people and middle-aged people. All these make for a familiar, comfortable place to worship. It is in the context of home and home church that I am my normal self; that I am who I know myself to be; that I am a person who has identity.

2. Impact of Entrance into a Nursing Home

What is it then that our parishioner faces when she first moves into a long-term care facility or nursing home? No matter how loving and caring and how needed is the facility into which the person moves, the impact is enormous. In the first place, the person does not move there because of good health. The person is sick—perhaps sicker than ever before in her life. Severely diminished health itself weakens a sense of self. A person moves because help is needed. But help is given on someone else's terms and there is a perception (accurate) of a loss of control. There is a wrench to one's very sense of humanness. The person looks around and sees not the strong and vigorous and mixed-age group of people seen at home and at church, but a very specific population of people who need varying degrees of long-term care. Perhaps for the first time the new resident sees people who have Alzheimer's disease, or other degenerative brain diseases. Certainly they see up close, and touch, and smell, and rub shoulders with people in various stages of decline or "disrepair." A roommate—a stranger—is usually assigned. Other strangers set rules and schedules.

The self (at least in its worst fears and terrors) sees itself mirrored in others whose lot is not to be envied. At the moment of entry into the frightening world of the nursing home, it must seem that there are many who are living out their days unproductively, without much consciousness of the world around them. In a *Newsweek* article, "My World Now: Life in a Nursing Home, from the Inside" (June 27, 1994, p. 11), Anna Mae Halgrim Seaver writes: "Most of us are aware of our plight—some are not. Varying stages of Alzheimer's have robbed several of their mental capacities. We listen to endlessly repeated stories and questions. We meet them anew daily, hourly or more often." The impact of entry can be rightly described as shocking and threatening to the self at the deepest levels. The self recoils.

3. *Anger, Uselessness, Loneliness*

Whatever the benefits of physical care in this new setting, the human spirit is likely to be stirred by anger toward the family and God, a sense of uselessness, and a highly personal and threatening loneliness.

Some anger toward family and God is almost inevitable. No matter how much the new resident knows that entrance into the long-term care facility is the only thing to do, there is some profound sense of abandonment. Anger toward the family is to be expected. And as the sense of God, the image of God, is born and nurtured in family and supported by familiar relationships, this sense of being abandoned by family somehow makes the universe untrustworthy. The human spirit is eroded at deep levels where the relationship with God is lived. "This is crazy," an old friend repeated time after time in her first weeks in a nursing home. "This is crazy. This is crazy."

There is commonly a sense of uselessness. What is it that we are going to do now, we who have spent so much of our life *doing*? Productivity measures the human in mass American culture, not only for those in the work-force but for the retired as well. Many retirees are quite busy, of course; and even if the scope of activity has, in the years before entrance into the nursing home, become limited to routine tasks of personal and house maintenance, the individual has probably, given decreasing energy, felt useful. But now there is nothing that needs to be done—meals are served, beds are made, rooms are cleaned, even the most personal of care is often in others' hands. Again Anna Seaver writes, "I don't much like some of the physical things that happen to us. I don't care much for a diaper. I seem to have lost the control acquired so diligently as a child. The difference is that I'm aware and embarrassed but I can't do anything about it." The feeling of uselessness is often acute; and with it a diminished sense of self deepens and the realization grows that unproductiveness goes hand-in-hand with being a burden to others.

Whatever the limitations of the nursing home, it is likely where the person will spend the rest of her days. It is up to her to adapt and to get on with life. This required adaptation is a task that belongs to the individual alone—no one but her can do it. This is experienced subjectively as loneliness and is highly threatening. A person embarks on the moral career of a nursing home resident with little or no wisdom (except negative) about what that means or how it is to be lived. Even hospitalization for a brief time, if that has been the experience, is no preparation for this life. A recent seminary graduate who studied with me was stationed in a church that has attached to it a self-care retirement home and a nursing home. A fine athlete in college, he is now in an advanced stage of MS. Before he left to take up his post he was told that because of his worsening condition he was to move directly into the nursing home. He has dealt with a lot of hard things in his four years of degeneration of MS, but the impact on him of this news was beyond support. He would have to adapt to this with his own resources, and the adaptation would be both forced on him and be a source of incredible loneliness. A similar impact occurs time and again on entrance into nursing homes.

In general (allowing for individual differences) the impact of this entrance is anger toward one's family and God, a sense of uselessness, and a forced adaptation that is highly personal and threatening. But the new resident must come to terms with the new reality.

4. *Reorganization and Adaptation*

The next phase is reorganization and adaptation as the resident struggles to adjust to a new environment and to reorder life in a new setting. The new environment is not like any environment one has known. It is not like going home again in a weakened state. It is not like moving. Its daunting task is to find a way of being oneself with beauty and integrity in a surrounding which is, in terms of anything for which the culture has prepared us, foreign. And because we are so much products of the culture which nourishes us and gives us identity, we have to learn to let go of some aspects of the very self we have loved. We have to search for a new self, a self that is not measured by physical strength, by the looks of or association with those who are young and vigorous, or by productiveness. We must find a new self that is measured by things that are closer to the heart of what it means to be human, although the culture with its high-noon vision of the human tells us otherwise.

The new resident has to search for a reason to be there but not by becoming productive again in any sense that will be easily understood by a self so profoundly marked by this culture. There has to be discovered a reason to be in this nursing home, whether that reason is perceived as an ability to help the worse-off neighbor or to pray for others or to relieve a burden from the family. For healthy adaptation the reason has to be strong enough and clear enough that the resident is able to be thankful to be in the nursing home. The reason has to be able to sustain the human spirit in a context far from anything ever known as home. The actual resolution may sound as undramatic as the way Anna Seaver ends her article: "This is my world now. It's all I have left. You see, I'm old. And, I'm not as healthy as I used to be. I'm not necessarily happy with it but I accept it."

It is an arduous and lonely struggle to come to a new relationship with the self, to decide how to relate to others. The new resident must find people with similar interests, a community of friends, friends unlike friends she/he knew before, but friends nonetheless. And the new resident must learn how to relate all over again to God.

B. Pastoral Care: "Teach Us To Pray"

In this section, we return our focus to the pastoral minister in relationship with the new nursing home resident, with emphasis on the pastoral role of helping the person to pray her way through to a new relationship with self and God. We then consider briefly what constitutes appropriate pastoral ministry with the family of the new resident. Finally we inquire about the mutual engagement of nursing home resident and congregation in ministry.

1. With the New Resident

A study of the perception of needs in three long-term care facilities compares the residents' understanding of their needs for pastoral care and that of their pastors. The residents said unanimously that what helped them move through impact and recoil to reorganization and adaptation was personal prayer. Their pastoral ministers, on the other hand, thought the need was for communal worship, for collective activities. While both ministers and residents agreed on the need for reassurance, for the re-creation of a meaningful life, and for a personal relationship with God, the residents reported that these needs were met "through pri-

vate and personal spiritual activity and deeper involve-
ment in the internal side of spirituality" (Lea Pardue,
*Models for Ministry: The Spiritual Needs of the Frail Elderly
Living in Long-Term-Care Facilities*. Ashville, NC: Mars Hill
College, 1989, p. 29).

The pastoral question, then, is what we can do to help
people develop the inner side of their lives of devotion. Or,
more simply, what is it that we can do to help new residents
in nursing homes to pray. Before addressing the specifics of
engaging in this pastoral task, it is well noted that we may
approach this task with a sense of unease, even of dread.
Why? To come close to the inner life of another in such a
moment of darkness puts to the test the adequacy of our
meditation on the mysteries of faith, puts to the test whether
our own psyche and souls are refined by fire, puts to the test
the quality of our own inner lives. What is needed by the
new resident is a guide whose specific qualifications are
rooted in a serious struggle with the same ultimate realities
and some sureness of knowledge about the inner life of
prayer.

What can you do to help people pray at this specific
moment of pastoral need? First, we can understand the
importance of personal prayer and the inner life for assurance, for the re-creation of a meaningful life, and for a new
relationship with God. (Concomitantly we must recognize
that communal activities are *not* what is needed.) If we
truly understand this, at least the new resident does not
have to apologize for what is happening or for the chosen
path for resolution.

Second, we can help by understanding what a difficult
task is the re-creation of meaning. Neither the culture nor
the church culture has an adequate sense of what it means
to grow old. To make sense of old age, frailty, sickness,
homelessness, and death is an unenviable burden.

Third, we can help unlink personal prayer and worship,

not simply by stepping back from the conviction that what is needed at this moment is collective worship, but by actively addressing the issue. Although this may seem to run contrary to the thrust of this book, it highlights how specific is this moment in the life of a nursing home resident, and how personal is the struggle to make a successful transition. People will say that they have prayed personal prayer, but in some measure this prayer has been supported by familiar people, familiar places, and familiar weekly rhythms of prayer. Now the places the resident prayed are no longer her places of prayer; and the self who prayed there is no longer the same self. The resident cannot go home again, physically or spiritually. There is a sense of uprootedness that needs to be articulated forthrightly. Only when it is named is it fair to add that it is possible to begin to pray again in this new old age.

Fourth, with those for whom these are issues, we must be able to contend with and to deal with the anger and the frustration toward God that may be part of the transition. Anger toward God is not a fashionable topic for sermons. But at this stage there will be a profound sense of disappointment in God, and for some a profound sense that life (that is, God and family) has cheated them. For others the emotion will be anger and then desolation—a sense that there is no consolation in God.

The classics of the spiritual life speak about the dark night of the senses and of the soul. One of the reasons we lift up minds and hearts to God is that we find certain consolation in it—a certain quietness, a certain wellness. The expectation that this is a legitimate outcome of prayer is fostered by a common assumption that prayer has something to do with feeling well about ourselves, so that we are not burdened by desolation, by no sense of center, by no sense of connectedness, by no sense of the mystery of the presence of God. John of the Cross writes: "Wishing to strip them of this old [person] and clothe them with the new...God divests the faculties, affection, and sense, both spiritual and sensory, interior and exterior. He leaves the intellect in darkness, the will in aridity, the memory in emptiness, and the affections in supreme affliction, bitterness, and anguish, by depriving the soul of the feeling and satisfaction it previously obtained from spiritual blessings" ("The Dark Night," in *John of the Cross: Selected Writings*. Mahwah, NJ: Paulist, 1987, p. 185).

In the face of these moments of desolation, when even the courage to will God's will seems repugnant, we need to approach our parishioner with understanding so that there will be no appeal to the old ways. People who are experiencing desolation in prayer do not need cheerful pray-ers who cannot be in silence themselves before the awful mystery of God. Entrance into a nursing home calls for massive reorganization of the self without many of the supports that hold one's self together, including the consolation of prayer. We have to be able to be with those who experience desolation or abandonment in silence. No word of consolation is appropriate; this is not a time of consolation. The struggle of the soul with God is intensely personal. Desolation may give way to a time of silence or quietness in prayer, to a new way of praying. To this we need to be attentive and supportive.

Then, finally perhaps, the nursing home resident may come to new life. John of the Cross writes of the new life that emerged from the dark night of the spirit: "One dark night, Fired with love's urgent longings—Ah, the sheer grace!—I went out unseen, my house being now all stilled."

2. With the Family

Where is the family in all this? The event is threatening at many levels. First, there is a sense of inadequacy, guilt, and secret relief when we have left a parent in a long-term care facility. "Could we not have kept mother at home a little longer....Think of all she did for us." Second, there is a sense of dread that we ourselves will someday be left in such a place. "I'd rather die than be in a place like that!"

Our ministry with the family is largely supportive. We give them a space in which they can talk through their fear, guilt, anger perhaps, and sense of dread. No quick response on our part can help. In fact, we could probably do nothing less helpful than say, "It's natural to feel like this. It's OK. This is best for your mother. Trust me!" People need time and support to work through these complex feelings. To be part of uprooting a loved parent from home, and to be party to putting her in a place where she is in such turmoil (whatever face she may put on it) is a burden not lightly put aside. The pressure may continue on the adult child for a long time. The resident may acknowledge that her children put her here for her own good. Without wanting to be a burden to them, she may be quite clear in her desire to see a lot of them. This can put a lot of pressure on the adult children, whose lives are very busy and whose feelings may be quite conflicted. In the face of this our ministry must be supportive, but not prescriptive or intrusive. We probably know relatively little of the patterns of love (or hurt) that specific families bring with them to this situation.

3. With the Congregation

Is there anything we can do beforehand to prepare people for this time of life? Clearly there are some things that can be done. If there is time and warning, parishioners can be helped to say goodbye to home, to neighborhood, and to church. Religious professionals are used to ritual leave-taking from a church they have served for five or ten years. Could we not find comparable rites of passage for parishioners who are leaving after twenty or thirty years? There must be a terrible poignancy if the last memory of one's home church is that nobody said goodbye.

Whether this is or is not possible for a specific individual, in general it is important to speak forthrightly about the realities of life in the nursing home. Sensitive (and blunt) descriptions of the *spiritual* struggles of the new nursing home resident is a powerful way to expand the notion of the human and to help us rethink the sacredness of all life. There is much to teach and learn. What is required is that we bring back not simply cheerful messages (or, worse, no messages at all), but stories of these often heroic struggles and successes in the life of the spirit—some of what they have learned about prayer, about life, about new identity, about new communication, about new friendship. Although the context is somewhat different, a wonderful testimony of the depth of human life in a long-term care facility is the book already noted by Ruth Howard Gray, *Survival of the Spirit: My Detour Through a Retirement Home*, written when the author was in her late eighties.

Nursing home residents have much to teach us. If we are unafraid to draw close, we have much to learn and thus to preach. The lessons have a pointedness that gives new meaning to religious convictions that all life is holy, and is part of God's gift. To speak of the giftedness of life is not to intimate that all life is equally friendly toward everyone. Sometimes as life passes on it doesn't seem to care much about some individuals. While life is gifted it is also burdened by its fickleness. The nursing home resident who has learned anew to thank God for this life can be a powerful teacher and witness.

4. Nursing Home Resident and Congregation Together

In this final section, we consider our role in empowering outreach from the congregation to the nursing home, and empowering the ministry of nursing home residents.

A. EMPOWERING OUTREACH TO A NURSING HOME

There are some patently bad strategies to avoid, first among which is taking unprepared people to a nursing home. The nursing home is a demanding environment, and good visitation requires both intentionality and preparation. In particular, but not exclusively, youth groups need *much* preparation if the visit is to be anything but a negative experience. Much of what we have already said may be helpful in preparing people for a visit that is creative, means something to the residents, and is likely to be repeated. This latter point is very important. People who are already isolated do not need the rejection of a one-time visit.

Positively, know your parishioners and select people for whom visitation may be a gift or talent. These gifts may be diverse. A friend takes a gentle dog to a nursing home weekly, to the delight to some residents who, like many of us, enjoy petting a friendly animal. Some parishioners may be good at telephoning a resident regularly. Others may be glad to help in worship. Yet others may be willing to have their prayer or study group meet at the nursing home. What we look for in selecting visitors is a sense that the visits will be ongoing and open to growth on all sides. If the visitor is impervious to change there can be little real communication.

B. EMPOWERING THE NURSING HOME RESIDENT

There are, for nursing home residents who are reasonably well, many opportunities for ministry to the larger church, as part of prayer circles, as part of a telephone support team, or within some other current church outreach. We have found in many nursing home residents a care, even a passion, for a wider world. At this time of life, the extent of outreach may be a letter to a senator about some need, or simply prayer for the city and world. All these are important parts of ministry within the body of Christ. Our role as ministers is to encourage, organize, and celebrate these gifts.

If we and our congregants learn from parishioners in the nursing home a sense of thanksgiving in difficult situations and the ability to celebrate life together, we will be engaged in nursing home ministry that is important for our personal and professional growth—however challenging, and however much it changes us all.

And so we conclude our reflections on pastoral visiting in the nursing home. Whatever the seriousness of these pages, we hope that, for you as for us, visiting in the nursing home brings memorable moments of joy, of shared triumph, of genuine and unforgettable grace.